BUILDERS AND PIONEERS
OF AUSTRALIA

When I was a King and a Mason—in the open noon of my pride
They sent me a Word from the Darkness—They whispered and
    called me aside.
They said—"The end is forbidden." They said—"Thy use is
    fulfilled,
And thy palace shall stand as that other's—the spoil of a King
    who shall build."

.   .   .   .   .   .

Only I cut on the timber, only I carved on the stone:
"After me cometh a Builder. Tell him I too have known!"

BUILDERS AND PIONEERS
OF
AUSTRALIA

BY
ARTHUR WILBERFORCE JOSE

Essay Index Reprint Series

originally published by
J. M. DENT & SONS LTD.

BOOKS FOR LIBRARIES PRESS
FREEPORT, NEW YORK

First Published 1928
Reprinted 1970

STANDARD BOOK NUMBER:
8369-1522-4

LIBRARY OF CONGRESS CATALOG CARD NUMBER:
71-107720

PRINTED IN THE UNITED STATES OF AMERICA

INTRODUCTION

THE history of the Australian Commonwealth—the most purely British nation in the British Empire, the mother-country herself not excepted—is almost unknown to the Empire at large, and in Australia is understood far too little. Most people know that it began as a convict settlement, and many think of it still as a colony of convicts' descendants blended with those of gold-diggers and of "remittance-men." Not so long before the Great War, Mr. Gilbert Chesterton told the world authoritatively that "we should no more dream of pitting Australian armies against German than of pitting Tasmanian sculpture against French"; yet Victorian sculptors (and Victoria is Tasmania's child) seem to rank high these days, and Ludendorff discovered the fighting value of an Australian army. One may therefore, without altogether undue presumption, hope that an attempt to account for this somewhat astonishing Commonwealth, which has mothered the Anzacs, created the first Dominion navy, and bred statesmen to match and encounter on equal terms the mother-country's ablest, will not lack interest for English readers to-day.

The most striking feature of Australian development is its apparent discontinuity. Those who first contemplated a settlement on the coast discovered by James Cook hoped to make it an adequate substitute for the lost colonies of the Atlantic border; Matra and Young saw in it a centre for trade with China, and an outpost against Dutch Malaysia and Spanish America. The British Government (and perhaps the East India Company) tore that scheme to tatters and decided on using Botany Bay as a rubbish-tip, where convicted rogues and other undesirables could be deposited at a convenient distance from the community that had produced them. The rubbish-tip scheme lasted some decades, and was expanded into a bogey scheme—Botany Bay was to be so terrible a gaol that criminals would be scared into good behaviour lest they should be sent to it. (That notion, whether by design or ill-luck, was afterwards embodied in the purely British gaols at Port Arthur and Norfolk Island, which—despite *For the Term of His Natural Life* and *It's Never Too Late to Mend*—were no more Australian than Dartmoor. It was in England, too, that the real bogeys developed, the hulks; it is recorded of a notable convict that, being sentenced to seven years in the hulks, he begged the judge to give him instead twice as long a term in New South Wales.)

The conversion of this rubbish-tip into a British colony, against all orders and all forms of hostile action, was the work of a great man, Lachlan Macquarie; his attempts to reconstruct it in detail were thwarted by the Colonial Office of the day as thoroughly as those of Matra and Young had been, but he at any rate abolished the bogey and the gaol. The New South Wales of the 1820's might have become a new Virginia, peopled by slave-driving landowners and their convict slaves; another great man, William Charles Wentworth, blocked that development, judiciously restrained the London-bred doctrinaire reformers of the 1830's, and gave the expanding settlements of coastal Australia an individuality that protected them against the grandmotherly solicitude of the Wakefields and Greys. Then came another sharp turn; Wentworth's ideals disappeared before the influx of cosmopolitan gold-seekers, and a third great man—I use the words deliberately of all three—devised from the

Introduction

bitter experiences of his own youth laws to suit and to breed free, homogeneous, British communities capable of mastering their Antipodean environment. Henry Parkes did more; convinced both by reason and experience that these free communities were neutralising each other as long as they refused to forget their petty mutual quarrels, he strove to harness them as a team and at least accustomed them to the idea, however distasteful it might be for the moment, of combined action. And the actual welding of the six discordances into a Commonwealth was, no less than the previous transformations, the work particularly of one man—Alfred Deakin.

Here, therefore, the development of the Commonwealth from gaol to Dominion is studied under the guise of four biographical sketches—of Macquarie, Wentworth, Parkes, and Deakin—which attempt to describe both the essential qualities and the idiosyncrasies of the men mainly responsible for Australia as we know her. Macquarie's super-reformatory, of course, is as dead as Wentworth's squatting aristocracy, and neither Parkes nor Deakin would recognise without some qualms the Commonwealth they were so eager to fashion. But each of the four mastered the Australia of his day at a critical moment; each in trying to reshape it according to his ideal at least saved it from being misshapen according to the notions of ill-informed oversea authorities, and left it much better equipped for progress along its own lines. Macquarie thwarted superiors who had hoped to maintain the terrifying gaol; Wentworth harried and defeated those who were enforcing and emphasising class-distinctions and the sleek dictatorships of Downing Street; Parkes like Æsop's storm, and Deakin like the sun, strove to make the colonists of the nineties discard their wretched provincial cloaks and know themselves for free citizens of a whole continent. Not one of the four has yet received the tribute of a worthy biography—though Walter Murdoch's *Alfred Deakin : a Sketch*, to which I owe a great deal, cannot be passed by lightly, its chief defect being its over-insistence on his purely Victorian and pre-Federation career.

The shorter sketches which follow are concerned mainly with pioneers and adventurers along various lines of Australian development whose work, though of real and lasting value, has been up to the present either almost unknown or sadly mis-remembered. The youngest student of Australian history knows something about Tasman the over-praised, and the great James Cook (who has found a good biographer), and John Macarthur (who badly needs one). How many of the most assiduous students know even the names of Jan Carstenszoon and John Blaxland and Simeon Lord? In this section of the book individual choice has been my guide. One may, I think, safely say that the four great Australian builders are the four here dealt with at some length. But among pioneers and lesser master-masons there is a very wide choice—there is Arthur Phillip for one, without whom Botany Bay would have become a derelict community of half-castes; there are the Busbys and the Cunninghams and the Dangars and the Greenes, Mitchell who gave New South Wales her roads and Lennox who built her bridges, gallant explorers, far-seeing merchants, undaunted adventurers without number. One can but use one's individual judgment; and I have chosen to revive the memories of those least remembered, because their story lies outside the range of the normal historical student.

My acknowledgments are due—as must be those of every student of Australian history—primarily to the magnificent collections of the Mitchell Library at Sydney, with which I made a close acquaintance when editing *The Australian*

Introduction

Encyclopædia; in the next place to that Encyclopædia itself, in which is accumulated much information not previously published. From the libraries of the British Museum, the Colonial Office, and the Royal Colonial Institute I have, of course, gained great advantage, both through the matter stored in them and through the courtesy of their librarians. It would be difficult to recall, and perhaps tedious to enumerate, all the no less courteous replies to private enquiries which have helped me to verify or correct details; I can only thank in general all who made those replies, and stress my thanks by adding that each separate enquiry elicited not only courtesy but zealous endeavour to hunt down the elusive fact into the last recesses of its hiding-place.

And I trust that Australia, for whose advantage and honour I have sought the truth about her history these many years, will not find my sketches of her founders and early lovers inadequate beyond reason.

A. J.

May, 1928.

CONTENTS

	PAGE
INTRODUCTION	v

THE BUILDERS

LACHLAN MACQUARIE	3
WILLIAM CHARLES WENTWORTH	36
HENRY PARKES	66
ALFRED DEAKIN	98

SOME PIONEERS

JAN CARSTENSZOON (Explorer)	127
JOHN BLAXLAND (Farmer)	141
GREGORY BLAXLAND (Farmer and Explorer)	154
SIMEON LORD (Merchant and Manufacturer)	167
FRANCIS HOWARD GREENWAY (Architect)	179
GEORGE HOWE (Printer and Journalist)	187
WILLIAM HILTON HOVELL (Explorer)	196
JAMES KING (Inventor and Viticulturist)	209
INDEX	215

MAPS

facing page

THE NEIGHBOURHOOD OF SYDNEY, SHOWING THE BELT OF RUGGED HILL-COUNTRY WHICH SURROUNDS IT	12
MAP OF THE COASTLINE OF NEW GUINEA AND NORTHERN AUSTRALIA, TO ILLUSTRATE CARSTENSZOON'S VOYAGE	132
MAP SHOWING THE EXPLORERS' TRACKS ACROSS THE BLUE MOUNTAINS	164
PLAN OF SYDNEY, 1823	180

THE BUILDERS

LACHLAN MACQUARIE

THE story of Australia's colonisation really begins in the second decade of the nineteenth century. A British seaman had annexed its eastern coast in 1770; another British seaman had in 1788 made there a settlement of prisoners and their guards; for the next twenty years this settlement had slowly grown into a collection of prison depots, all situated close to the coast, none more than forty miles deep inland, escape from which was deliberately made difficult by the choice of locations guarded by almost impenetrable bush on the land side and the immense expanse of the Pacific Ocean otherwise. The Governors were first of all captains of warships; the force through which they maintained order among their prisoners was a nominally military body raised for that special purpose, with no military traditions, including in its ranks many ex-prisoners, and officered for the most part by young moneyed men who spent their time chiefly in speculation on the scanty crops, or on the infrequent consignments of merchandise that reached Port Jackson. There were, of course, better men among them—officers who had seen service and imbibed military traditions in the British army—nor were the rank and file, whatever their origin, unworthy of their trust. But the majority of the officers were selfish, arrogant, undisciplined disturbers of the order which such a settlement so badly needed; and the bitter quarrels that repeatedly broke out between them and the several Governors made New South Wales a place to be avoided by free colonists, and contemned by any man who, in those years of struggle against Napoleon, had a thought to spare for British expansion oversea.

When in 1808 this pseudo-military clique topped off its pretensions with a mutiny against the last naval Governor, William Bligh, the authorities in London were forced into action. It may have been Castlereagh, then in charge of the War and Colonial departments—it may have been William Wellesley-Pole (afterwards Lord Mornington), then Secretary of the Admiralty, who for some reason did a good deal of the New South Wales correspondence—one of these two, at any rate, noted with keen eye the root of the evil, and determined to substitute for the naval Governor dependent on semi-military aid a military Governor commanding a regiment which could be trusted to obey him. In London there was no design to alter the nature of the settlement; all Castlereagh or Wellesley-Pole wanted was to restore and secure order in the distant gaol. But the choice they made among their available officers was fateful.

The first man chosen was Brigadier-General Nightingall, a gallant soldier with a good record in India and a meed of just-earned praise from Sir Arthur Wellesley for his work at the battle of Vimeiro; he was also a protégé of Lord Cornwallis, whose influence at the moment was particularly dominant. Why Nightingall should have wanted the post is not clear, but his health was always poor, and he may have hoped that a long sea voyage and sojourn in a sunnier country would set him up again. As it was, his malady returned upon him too soon, and he was forced to resign the post before he could take it up. The War Office, asked for a regiment to accompany him, had suggested the 73rd—

its reasons again are obscure. All arrangements had been made to move it before Nightingall fell ill, the Government was far too busy with bigger affairs to spare more time for New Holland, and the simplest way out of the difficulty was to give the Governorship to the commanding officer of the regiment, who would under other conditions have been at any rate Lieutenant-Governor. So, by a series of mishaps and hasty decisions, Australia obtained the services of a statesman.

This is not to say that Lachlan Macquarie, the new choice, was up to that time undistinguished. So well known already was he that John Macarthur, an Australian colonist who had recently reached England, could write:

> If he prove on trial at all equal to the universal character he has here, his government cannot but prove a blessing to the colony.

His previous career, indeed, though it had not been what men in those fighting days called "brilliant," had afforded him many opportunities of showing both cool courage and great administrative ability. He was born on Ulva off Mull in Argyll on 31 January, 1761, and may as a boy have helped to entertain Samuel Johnson,[1] who in 1773 visited his father, Lauchlan Macquarrie, the last chief of "a Clan not powerful nor numerous, but of antiquity which most other families are content to reverence." He entered the army in 1777, saw service during the American Revolution

---

[1] Johnson was much interested in the old chief, the only Highlander who still had the *Mercheta Mulierum*, commuted in his case to a fine of a sheep or a crown-piece for every girl married within his dominion. When in 1777 Macquarrie had to sell his share of Ulva, Boswell urged Johnson to buy Little Colonsay and establish on it a Church of England school.

B

in Nova Scotia, New York and South Carolina, was commissioned captain in 1788 and sent with the 77th to India (where he was in the fighting against Tippoo Sahib at Cannanore and Seringapatam), helped to annex the Dutch settlements at Cochin and in Ceylon, and went through the second siege of Seringapatam in 1799. Next year he was appointed deputy-adjutant-general to David Baird, then in command of an Indian contingent that was to co-operate with Abercromby in sweeping up the remains of Bonaparte's Egyptian expedition; he saw the capitulation of Alexandria, was made a major in 1801, returned to India, and for eighteen months was military secretary to Jonathan Duncan, the Governor of Bombay. In 1803 he obtained leave, went back to England, and was appointed assistant-adjutant-general for the London district; in 1805 Duncan reclaimed him, and—although in May of that year he was gazetted lieutenant-colonel of the 73rd, which was about to return from India to Europe—he remained with Duncan till the end of 1806. Then, after an adventurous journey up the Persian Gulf and across Persia, Armenia and Russia, he once more reached London in October 1807, and was sent to Perth to join his regiment.

The man, therefore, who was to become the founder of a British colony in Australia had nurtured himself on three impressive traditions—the chieftainship of a Highland clan, the martial ardour of a fighting career, and the sober control of administrative experience. He was proud, he was brave, he was wisely masterful. He found himself by sheer accident set down at the ends of the earth to restore order to a community of mutinous officials and half-despondent, half-desperate convicts; so long as order was maintained and expenses kept down, he would sufficiently please his superiors in London. Meanwhile, his former comrades might be winning laurels with Wellington in Spain — as indeed many of his successors did.

On 8 May, 1809, Macquarie was commissioned Governor of New South Wales, on the 22nd he sailed with his regiment, and on 28 December, seven months out, saw first the towering headland that forms Port Jackson's northern portal. Uncertain of the local situation—for no one in England had been able to tell him much about either the temper of the mutineer-ruled settlement or the whereabouts of the deposed Governor—he lay just inside the Heads for a couple of days, studied the surroundings and digested the settlement's news; on the 30th he moved six miles up the harbour to Sydney Cove, and at noon on 1 January, 1810, assumed control of affairs with all possible solemnity, by way of symbolising to his new and unruly subjects the re-establishment of unbreakable discipline. Scanning him with furtive and suspicious eyes, they saw "a clean-shaven, strong, vigorous-looking man, about 5 ft. 10 in. in height, nearly 14 stone in weight; he has a swarthy skin and dark gray, penetrating eyes beneath compelling brows, which knit under excitement." Clearly a man not to be trifled with—nor was he, ever.

He had been instructed in London to reinstate the deposed Bligh before assuming office himself, but this was rendered impossible by the ex-Governor's own conduct. For nine months of 1809 he had been lying off Hobart in Tasmania aboard his gun-brig, the *Porpoise*, unable to land because the local administrator took orders from the Sydney authorities, mutineers though they were, and unwilling to leave Australian waters as a refugee. When he heard of Macquarie's arrival in Port Jackson, he took the *Porpoise* north again, joined Macquarie on 17 January, and spent nearly four months in Sydney accumulating evidence to be produced against his deposers (who had been or were being sent to London for trial), and incidentally making himself a nuisance both to the new Governor and to the usually gentle and tactful Mrs. Macquarie. However, Sydney was heartily sick of irregular domination and of all parties to the recent trouble, and Macquarie found himself in full accord with public feeling when he shipped off to England the old semi-military "New South Wales Corps," and with them, or in advance of them, all civilians whom Bligh chose to designate either as guilty participants in the mutiny or as necessary witnesses on his side.

The tables thus cleared, he sat down (but not for long) to think out his future policy. Two things struck him at once —the discomfort and disorder of the settlement's physical organisation, and the remarkable ability and civic capacity of some of the men still classed as convicts. He had as yet no further ambition than to ensure comfort and order among his new subjects, and perhaps to give the best of them a fair chance of redeeming the follies or errors of their past career. To begin with, he instituted a building programme of some magnitude, requisitioned London for a competent surveyor and architect, and began to replan the dirty and straggling town that twenty years of unsupervised individualistic hut-construction had given him for a capital. For the first time Sydney found itself endowed with comparatively straight streets, each named and graded, with a market square, a recreation ground, and a common for grazing stock. The 73rd, a regiment with traditions and self-respect, needed and obtained new barracks; the convicts who were to be kept in Sydney for carrying out the works programme must have clean barracks too, and a good hospital, and sound granaries for their food-stores.

So much for the central settlement; what now of the

outlands, which must learn to feed the whole community? Macquarie in the late spring of his first year (November–December) made a round of his dominions. In thirty-seven days he had surveyed the whole by horse or boat, determined the sites of five new townships, considered the capabilities of each district for stock-raising or wheat-growing, and procured from the few settlers who were really in earnest about their work advice for improving the Government farm. In 1811 he extended his travels to Hobart, and the Tasmanian capital underwent a rearrangement like that of Sydney, with plans for barracks and a hospital there also. Building, as we shall have opportunities to note, was Macquarie's chief passion. For Tasmania — then and for many years to be known only as Van Diemen's Land—he had little more to do. For the main settlement his best work as an expander—a *Mehrer des Reichs*—was yet to come. His month in 1810 had left him convinced that nothing important could be done while the settlement was still a prison with a few square miles of market-garden and pasture-land attached. That had been the ideal of the naval Governors, accustomed to keep order within narrow limits, and to depend on outside help for their provisions. Bligh, for instance, had never understood why Macarthur and his fellows should want large areas on which to breed sheep, and had been inordinately proud—as a sailor cast away on a desert island would be—of growing a few potatoes and making the settlement temporarily self-supporting in cereals; and Bligh, who, after all, did take an interest in manures and in clean farming, was by far the best of the naval men in matters concerned with agriculture. Moreover, the districts best suited to farming were also most liable to flooding, and few precautions could be taken against that sudden and deadly danger. But at the best, when there had been no floods for three years together, Macquarie could only report in 1812 that out of 150,000 acres nominally occupied less than 10,000 were under wheat; less than 7000 were under other crops, about the same area lying fallow, and the remainder used to run sheep and a few cattle. This was no solid foundation for the prosperity of 12,000 people.

The story of Gregory Blaxland's adventure along the contorted knife-edge of the Blue Mountains is told elsewhere in this volume. Here we need only remember that it was Macquarie's support and encouragement that set him going, and Macquarie's active brain that saw at once the possibilities of the new discovery (which in itself was limited) and devised means to utilise it. Blaxland was back in Sydney in June of 1813; by November Macquarie had Surveyor Evans afield, in December the rich valley of the westward-flowing Macquarie had been found, in July 1814 William Cox was at work on a road along the knife-edge, and in April 1815 the Governor with a large party rode the 120 miles that separated Sydney from the new territory, and founded the first inland township, Bathurst. Under the conditions and with the instruments available to him, Macquarie had already deserved well of his country. But admiration is due to his foresight as well as to his energy. He had secured the territory necessary for legitimate expansion; he determined that it should not be at once handed over to the seekers for pasture, who would occupy large areas of soil fit for closer cultivation. Wherefore he began by forbidding all western settlement, except for half a dozen labourers whom he planted at Bathurst to cultivate two acres each by way of experiment; and he sought (and gained) approval from Earl Bathurst — then and for another twelve years in charge of Colonial affairs—for a scheme whereby all the river-flats should be gradually partitioned into small farms of fifty to one hundred acres each, pasture-seekers being relegated to the bordering foothills, where there was plenty of grass but cropping conditions were less favourable. And to all western grants, as to those of land or town lots in the seaboard area, he applied strict conditions of sale. No grantee might alienate within five years of the date of his grant; during that five years a defined area of land must be cleared and cultivated; if the grant was of a town lot, a two-story building must be erected, fifty feet by sixteen; if the town lot was only leased, then a house thirty-six feet by fourteen must be erected within three years. There was a deal of grumbling about these conditions, and several appeals to London; but Macquarie was right and was (for the time) sustained, and it would have been well for New South Wales if his policy had been continued by his successors.

Administrative work is of so varied a character that it would be confusing to deal with it chronologically; one cannot sandwich in Macquarie's achievements as a builder and settler among his dealings with convicts and aborigines and his quarrels with recalcitrant magistrates and jealous landowners. We will consider him first as a constructor—of roads, of buildings, of civilised settlements in the raw, unmanageable bush. Sydney, when he reached it in 1810, was the dilapidated centre of a very ramshackle community. Foveaux had been working at it for eighteen months, but with inadequate means and curtailed authority. The colony had no local treasury from which to defray working expenses, but had to finance everything by bills on the British Government, which—in the middle of the Napoleonic wars—Britain hated to pay. Worse, there were very few artisans or skilled labourers of any kind among the convicts. For some years Macquarie found himself compelled to let public works out by private contract. As this system placed him at the mercy of the contractors, who could demand almost any kind of payment they liked, he had on several occasions to pay them with privileges or monopolies. The most notorious example is that of the "Rum Hospital," which was built by Simeon Lord, D'Arcy Wentworth, and Garnham Blaxcell under a contract that gave them a three-years' monopoly of imported liquors; they paid a high duty on them, but the profit they reaped may be gauged by the fact that spirits sold during the monopoly at 30s. a gallon could be bought for 17s. the year after it expired. Much criticism has been wasted on this transaction, which in normal conditions would no doubt have been indefensible, but derives its justification from its circumstances; when the only hospital available for nearly 12,000 people is a ruinous wooden shed, a Governor needs little excuse for taking almost any legal means to provide a better building. From 1815 onwards, however, the port dues collected at Sydney and the local revenue from minor sources so increased that Macquarie was able to enter on a programme of public works almost entirely constructed under his own control, and his achievement became stupendous. By 1821 he could point to eighty miles of turnpike road linking up the townships east of the Blue Mountains, eighty miles of carriage road ("not yet turnpike") in the same district, one hundred and one miles of carriage road over the range to Bathurst, and fifteen miles of road suitable for the passage of artillery from Sydney to the coast. He endowed his capital with several public parks—which still exist as the Botanical Gardens, the Domain, Hyde Park, etc.—and experimental farms, one of which now surrounds the university. He built imposing stables for a Government House on the hill facing Port Jackson; the house itself he had intended to

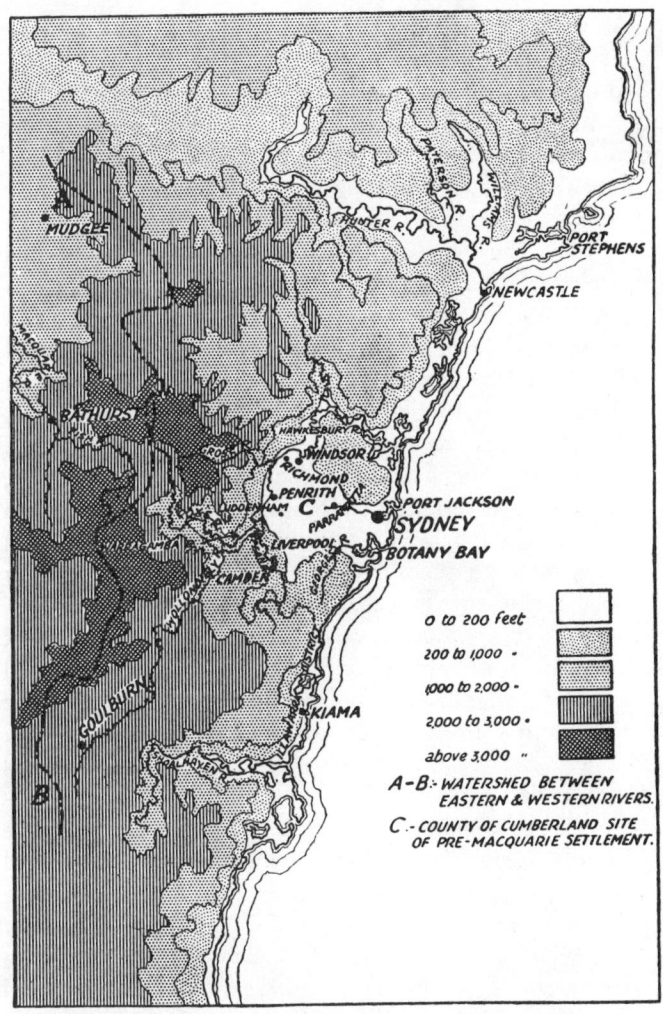

THE NEIGHBOURHOOD OF SYDNEY, SHOWING THE BELT OF
RUGGED HILL-COUNTRY WHICH SURROUNDS IT

erect on the ridge above (where the Mitchell Library now stands), but Bathurst forbade the expenditure; a Governor's country residence he built at Parramatta. Besides the "rum" hospital, he put up a military hospital in Sydney and four general hospitals in the bigger country townships (Parramatta, Windsor, Liverpool and Newcastle); a second church in Sydney and four in the townships, as well as six "chapels" in smaller settlements, all of them complete with parsonage and cemetery; four military barracks in Sydney and nine in the country; four barracks for convicts in Sydney and ten in the country; residences for the principal officials of the colony; a lighthouse at South Head, a fort [1] in Port Jackson, wharves there and at Windsor and Newcastle, court-houses at Sydney and Windsor, two lunatic asylums, a cattle hospital, and a water-supply for Parramatta. Many of these buildings are still in use. The main building of the rum hospital is now replaced by a more splendid and effective hospital, but one of its wings houses the New South Wales Legislature, and the other a year ago was housing the Sydney Mint. St. James's Church in Sydney and several of the country churches still function; the biggest convict barracks accommodates a district court and several Government law offices; the military hospital has become the State's most important school; the stables Macquarie built for his Government House have been converted to a Conservatorium of Music. This long list of public works may seem over-elaborated (though only the most important have been mentioned), but is needed both to justify the epithet "stupendous" and to explain to the reader the consternation with which Bigge in 1819 and the Colonial Office in 1821 regarded its Governor's grandiose achievements. They had no dream of an oversea Dominion; all

[1] For this fort see also *Greenway, Francis*, later in this volume.

they wanted was a receptacle for convicts—and, mayhap, for adventurous or superfluous younger sons—administered with the maximum of discipline and the minimum of expense; and there was disclosed to them a vision of vast spaces they had no use for and an administrative mechanism (still to some extent only sketched out, thank Heaven!) they could not at the moment afford. Little wonder that they seized on Bigge's sincere but narrow criticisms and Marsden's bitter calumnies as excuses for cancelling or pigeon-holing as many as possible of Macquarie's intended developments—or that his successors were encouraged to relieve the mother-country of all possible expenditure by distributing agricultural land wholesale [1] among pastoralists who would undertake to support convicts in return for their labour.

While utilising and organising the areas contiguous to Sydney, the Governor spared no pains to extend his sphere of action. His arrival at Bathurst in May 1815 was merely the prelude to further explorations during which Evans discovered the Lachlan. In 1817 Evans and his superior officer, John Oxley, were sent to follow the Lachlan down, but found themselves blocked by impenetrable swamps just when (though they did not know it) they were within two days' journey of the Murrumbidgee and of a clear passage to Encounter Bay. In 1818 the two were again dispatched westwards, followed the Macquarie till it, too, was lost in swamps, and then struck as nearly east as possible

[1] When Macquarie left Australia, about 40,000 people were settled on less than 600,000 acres; six years later, 62,000 were occupying 3,000,000 acres. Ninety years later, immigrants in search of farm-lands were still compelled to traverse for 200 miles fertile valley-land locked up in pastures before reaching inferior districts that were open for agriculture. Macquarie's regulations (see p. 11 above) would have prevented this scandal.

Lachlan Macquarie

for hundreds of miles across country until they came out on the precipitous edge of the main range two hundred miles north of Port Jackson, and descended to the rich, secluded river-flats of Port Macquarie.

These were official explorations, since they were directed into unknown and distant regions. Nearer home the Governor left such discovery to private venturers, encouraging them with grants of land and minor aid in their outfits. Thus Hamilton Hume—afterwards one of the discoverers of the upper Murray valley and of the overland route to Port Phillip—learnt his business by repeated journeys into the rough southern hill-country below Camden, and with Charles Throsby opened a track (by which the main Sydney-Melbourne railway line now runs) to the Goulburn Plains and the coast below the Illawarra. Throsby in other journeys linked these southern areas with Bathurst, and just before Macquarie resigned his governorship penetrated what is now the Federal Capital Territory. Government aid in several of these journeyings was typified by the attachment of James Meehan—one of Macquarie's favourite emancipists, and an excellent surveyor—to Hume's or Throsby's party, and the Governor himself delighted to mark his approval of the results by making in 1820 an official excursion to Lake George. The net result of all this exploration was that, whereas in 1810 New South Wales was a settled patch of barely two thousand square miles, and a Parliamentary Committee of 1812 reported that the extreme limits of the colony could not exceed sixty miles inland and one hundred and fifty along the coast, by 1821 its known area extended four hundred miles inland and about three hundred miles north and south.[1]

[1] Macquarie's term of office was also notable for the coastal explorations of Philip King, who between 1817 and 1822 charted

This expansive programme of works and explorations did not altogether distract the Governor's attention from the more immediate duties of a fatherly administration. Already occupied with the welfare of future generations, he began his career as chieftain of this motley clan with the re-endowment and reform of a girls' orphan school that had been in existence since Governor Hunter's time, and by establishing similar schools for both sexes at Sydney and Parramatta. Attempts to reform the morals of the adult convict population had to be confined mainly to exhortations, delivered both to those already in the colony and to new arrivals before they were disembarked. But marriage was as far as possible enforced instead of the prevalent concubinage, and Sunday observance was restored after many years of almost complete disuse; liquor sales were forbidden between 10 a.m. and 12.30 p.m., Sunday labour was prohibited as "shameful and indecent," and great stress was laid on the regular attendance at church services of all prisoners, both those employed and housed by the Government at Sydney or Parramatta and those assigned to settlers in the country districts. Marsden, the senior Church of England chaplain, and a few of his friends up-country protested strongly against the compulsory Sunday muster, alleging that the gangs thus brought together sadly misused the hours after service was over. The allegation was perhaps excusable on occasion; but it was even then characteristic of Marsden to find fault with anything Macquarie might propose.

the greater part of the northern and western coasts of Australia and added a good deal of detail to the existing charts of the eastern coast. But this was mainly Admiralty work in areas not at the time within the British sphere, and was not directly inspired or spontaneously aided by Macquarie himself.

For the aborigines, then still numerous in the precincts of Sydney, he had a good deal of misdirected affection, but there was no one in those days to guide him more wisely. Like most Englishmen of the time, he tried to treat them as Englishmen of a slightly less intelligent species. His first proclamation pointed out gravely and reasonably that their regrettable habit of carrying on tribal and personal war in close proximity to the settlements was disturbing, and would no longer be tolerated. This producing no effect, an expedition was dispatched into the blackfellow "marches" to shift the quarrelsome tribes farther away. When the expedition returned with four piccaninnies among its prisoners, Macquarie promptly founded a school for them, and in 1814 moved it, enlarged, to a site still named Blacktown—though by 1825 the school and its appurtenant buildings were already in ruins. Simple methods of agriculture were included in the training, and in 1821 two blackfellow boys were married to two of their schoolmates and granted farms and implements at Government expense. Not by such means, however, was the aboriginal problem to be settled. The essence of it was the unavoidable proximity of wild tribes, that lived by hunting, to settlers almost as wild who ran cattle and sheep on the tribes' old hunting-grounds. With the best will in the world collisions could not be avoided; when the unruly farm-occupants who infested the borderlands of civilisation chose to madden themselves with their own illicit brew of raw alcohol, collisions became frequent and brutal. Macquarie more than once found himself obliged to put down by armed force an aboriginal rising for which no one could justifiably blame the aborigines. Apart from the Blacktown experiment he seems to have had no constructive policy in this connection, though towards the end of his term he favoured (in principle) a proposal made by one of the colonial chaplains, Robert Cartwright; this was to establish a tribal reserve in the rough hill-country between the Nepean and the Warragamba, where hunting was still good, to let the adults do what they liked there, and to attract the children to schools where they might be taught handicrafts. Judging by much more recent experiences in South and Western Australia, this policy would have effected much good. But Macquarie was by that time weary, and only anxious to avoid more friction with his superiors in London over excessive expenditure, and could not bestir himself to initiate new schemes for anything.

There remains to be discussed the policy that was nearest the Governor's heart, at once his pride and his fatal stumbling-block—his treatment of ex-convicts who had either been pardoned or had served their time. As we have seen, almost his first impression of the colony convinced him of the civic value of several of these freed men, in contrast with the selfishness and arrogance of the military clique and its few free friends. In April 1810, Redfern the surgeon, Lord the merchant, and Andrew Thompson the Hawkesbury farmer, were already normal visitors at Government House, along with D'Arcy Wentworth, whom everyone in those days seems to have classed as an ex-convict. Macquarie made no secret of his attitude, and at first it was warmly applauded in London. The Parliamentary Committee on Transportation that sat in 1812 summarised his declarations in this respect, adding:

In these principles Your Committee cordially concur, and are the more anxious to express their views, as under a former Governor transports,[1] whatever their conduct might be, were in no instance permitted to hold places of trust and confidence, or even to come to the Government House.

---

[1] i.e. transported convicts. The Governor was Bligh.

Almost at the same moment Macquarie was re-formulating for Bathurst the principle he had in 1810 stated to Castlereagh, that the mere fact that the colony "was Originally Settled for the Reception, Punishment, and eventual Improvement of Convicts, appears to me to require that their Improvement, Welfare, and Happiness should form the first and Chief Object of Attention." In the following year, when opposition to his policy was showing itself both in Australia and in London, he became more insistent:

> Once a Convict has become a Free Man, either by Servitude, Free Pardon, or Emancipation, he should in All Respects be Considered on a Footing with every other Man in the Colony, according to his Rank in Life and Character. . . . No Doubt, many of the Free Settlers (if not all) would prefer (if it were left to *their* choice) never to admit persons who had been Convicts to any Situation of Equality with themselves. But in My humble Opinion in Coming to New South Wales they Should Consider that they are Coming to a Convict Country, and if they are too proud or too delicate in their feelings to associate with the Population of the Country, they should Consider it in time and bend their Course to some other Country.

This letter crossed on the ocean a warning from Bathurst that might, if given earlier, have softened the Governor's determination. He approved of some favour to emancipists, but thought magistracies a little above the deserts of the best of them, or at any rate inadvisable for the moment. As for admitting them to the Governor's table and requiring free settlers and military men to accept them as equals—

> As those who have been desirous of counteracting your Measures, have selected the Admission of Convicts into Society as their main point of Resistance, you will I am sure see the Necessity of not compromising your Authority by exerting it on a Subject, where Resistance may be so well cloaked under a rigid Sense of Virtue or a Refinement of Moral Feeling.

Wise advice; indeed, Bathurst was in all respects but one the wisest adviser and the soundest supporter Macquarie ever had. He failed in vision; he could not share the dreams in which Macquarie—and not he only: Phillip had dreamt them before him—foresaw a greater Australia. How should he? he was busied with the fate of Europe, the safeguarding of Napoleon, the restoration of a victorious but impoverished Britain to her heritage of world-wide power; he was shut in with the fogs, physical and intellectual, of a North Atlantic climate and of European diplomacy, and got no breath of the clear Pacific winds, no glow from the brilliant skies, that warmed Macquarie (and many great visionaries after him) like draughts of noble wine. Bathurst's special virtue, in Australian eyes, was this—though he sympathised scarcely at all with Macquarie's aims and hopes, he valued the man highly; his reprimands were directed against particular errors, never against the administration as a whole; and despite great pressure from his own subordinates, he maintained the Governor in power until that weary Titan had himself twice demanded his recall.

The warning of 1814, however, came too late. Macquarie had from the first set before himself an ideal—the creation, from the unpromising material supplied to him, of a new Britain in the Pacific. With this in view, it was all-important that whatever good material there was should be segregated from the dross and made to feel its own worth. "This is a convict colony," he said to himself; "very well, we will create an aristocracy of merit among the convicts"; and the most immediately valuable method of doing this was to secure recognition by the official and military cliques of the new aristocracy's status. Before Bathurst's warning was received he had angered Marsden by coupling with him on a road-board two emancipists whom the chaplain chose to consider immoral; he had quarrelled with Ellis Bent—an excellent and conciliatory official when he was not under his brother Jeffery's influence—over the admission of emancipists to Government House hospitality; he was on the verge of a quarrel with Jeffery Bent over the admission of emancipists to practise as attorneys before the Supreme Court. He had gone too far to take Bathurst's good advice, and withdrawal in 1815 would have both hurt his Scottish pride and gravely weakened his authority as Governor. Yet this failure does not necessarily carry with it a condemnation of Macquarie's ideal. It implies only that the ideal was not shared by those with whose help he had to work. His mistake —surely excusable, considering his extreme isolation—was to deal with New South Wales as a community existing for its own sake, not as an outlying appendage to a great European State. His superiors in London thought of it as a rubbish-heap on which to discharge offensive matter, and of him as a farm-hand detailed to keep the heap as sanitary and inconspicuous as possible. Most of his free subordinates in the colony also thought of it as a rubbish-heap, from which they might disinter useful matter; those who, like Macarthur and the Blaxlands, were not solely concerned with their own aggrandisement were at best interested in the development of particular methods of increasing its material prosperity. Between them Macquarie, his eyes fixed on the future, grew every year more isolated, more autocratic, more desperately avid of help and encouragement from any quarter.

Too much discussion has been wasted over Macquarie's disputes with his local subordinates. As Macarthur justly said, it was not his lot "to do that which I think no man ever will do, to give satisfaction to all." Apart from minor and personal grievances—such as his cavalier treatment of

c

the Blaxlands, and the neglect to bestow some special favour on Nicholas Bayly, which seems to have resulted from the miscarriage of a letter—the chief ground of complaint against him was his emancipist policy, which has just been dealt with. His misfortune was that it embittered not only the officers of several British regiments, who were only temporarily stationed in the colony and could carry tales to London when they left, but also the remarkable personality of Samuel Marsden,[1] one of the most self-contradictory characters of his or any day. Marsden's real grievance against the Governor is undiscoverable. Macquarie's rebuke to him for altering at his own free will the liturgy of the Established Church (an offence more serious then than it is to-day) hardly accounts for it. His work in New Zealand Macquarie aided whole-heartedly, though he did not return the compliment by helping Macquarie with the Australian aborigines. A fierce but not inexcusable attack made on him by the Governor's secretary in 1817 was rather the result than

[1] Marsden's missionary work in New Zealand, marked by courage and self-sacrifice of a high order, has blinded most of those who have written about him to his hopelessly inconsistent management of his own and his Church's affairs in New South Wales. There he was unquestionably a harsh magistrate, an unscrupulous politician, an avid money-maker. Bigge called him "less sensible than he ought to be to the impropriety of combining operations of a mercantile nature with the duties of his profession"; Brisbane stigmatised his "daily neglect of the spiritual concerns of his parish for the sake of attending to his own multitudinous temporal concerns"; Macarthur, unrestrained by any official tendency to euphemisms, wrote plainly: "Honest Sam Marsden has displayed more than his accustomed activity in propagating the most diabolical falsehoods." Macquarie's biographer, when he makes his appearance, may safely claim that any statements made on Marsden's authority need severe examination before they can be repeated.

the cause of ill-feeling. However it may be, Marsden was undoubtedly the central figure of the colonial opposition, and the instigator of the worst charges. But neither he nor any discontented settler or officer could have done much harm had not the Colonial Office itself been a hotbed of intrigue. Why, no one has yet discovered; but certain it is that by 1816 Henry Goulburn, Bathurst's right-hand man, was already intriguing for Macquarie's recall and for the appointment of Sir Thomas Brisbane in his place. He tested Macarthur on the subject; the complaints made against Macquarie, he said, were fully as serious as those long since made against Bligh. Macarthur refused to be inveigled. "Governor Macquarie," he told Goulburn, "is a gentleman in manners, humane, and friendly to all, at least to all who will take the trouble to recommend themselves to his favour, a man of unblemished honor and character." Goulburn answered sourly that Macarthur's answer was a proper one; but the rumour that Brisbane would shortly proceed to New South Wales was soon spread abroad in colonially interested circles. Nothing, it would seem, but Bathurst's personal support saved Macquarie then; if Bathurst could be shaken, the intrigue was sure of success.

Goulburn's opportunity was already within reach. Benjamin Vale, an assistant chaplain, had in 1815 for some reason taken on himself to seize a United States schooner at a Sydney wharf as lawful prize. Macquarie, who was out of Sydney at the moment, when he returned released the schooner, arrested Vale, and had him courtmartialled; the court sentenced him to a public reprimand, but Macquarie, for the sake of the culprit's sacred character, made the reprimand private. Vale, disregarding the courtesy, made complaint to the Colonial Office, and Goulburn drafted a severe rebuke to the Governor, pointing out that chaplains could be court-martialled only for offences involving their character—i.e. those of an immoral nature; he hoped, if we may believe Macarthur, that the severity would drive Macquarie to resign. Macquarie's first answer, sent on 24 November, 1817, was merely a strong protest against the rebuke, since Vale's interference in secular concerns was derogatory to his chaplaincy and therefore "scandalous and vicious"; but on second thoughts he fell into Goulburn's trap, and on 1 December tendered his resignation as Governor because of a "sudden change in your Lordship's Sentiments towards me." Bathurst, who had no intention of losing a good Governor for a technical illegality, answered the first protest by pointing out that, whatever the equities of the case, the court-martial was illegal, and therefore it was "impossible for me to express, on this instance, that approbation of your Conduct, which I have so often had the Gratification of conveying to You." The resignation he parried on 18 October, 1818, by offering Macquarie an opportunity of reconsidering it; "the whole Tenor of my communications on the subject of the Colony," he added, and justly, "has been to uphold your proper authority."

Unfortunately, this fair and friendly letter never reached its addressee. One cannot produce definite evidence against anyone, but it may be surmised that somewhere in the anti-Macquarie cabal courage was found to intercept it. Meanwhile, another grievance came to hand. In 1816 three men and a woman, all of bad character, but one man (Blake) a free man, had been caught trespassing on the Governor's private grounds against strict orders, and probably for immoral purposes. Macquarie ordered them twenty-five lashes each. Jeffery Bent, Marsden, and others of their clique, took the men's affidavits, reported the affair to

London, and briefed a member of the House of Commons to attack the Governor violently for this outrage on a free man. A petition was got up for presentation to Parliament, coupling the Vale case with the Blake case, and Macquarie made things worse for himself by cancelling privileges he had granted to one of the petitioners. Faced with all these complaints, new and old, Bathurst was forced to slacken his support of the accused Governor and compromise on an inquiry; and instead of a reply, favourable or other, to his proffered resignation, that much-enduring and expectant man received early in 1820 a dispatch (already nearly twelve months old) which announced the appointment of a Special Commissioner to investigate the affairs of the colony. Worse still, it was to be judged not as a growing colony, but as a probably inefficient gaol — "more particularly with a view of ascertaining how far in its present improved and increasing State, it is susceptible of being made adequate to the Objects of its original Institution." This note was repeated in Bigge's instructions, a copy of which was forwarded with the dispatch:

The Settlements in New Holland . . . not having been established with any view to Territorial or Commercial Advantages, must chiefly be considered as Receptacles for Offenders. . . . So long as they continue destined by the Legislature of the Country to these purposes, their Growth as Colonies must be a Secondary Consideration, and the leading Duty of those to whom their Administration is entrusted will be to keep up in them such a system of just discipline as may render Transportation an Object of serious Apprehension. . . . The first Object of your Enquiry should be to ascertain whether any and what Alteration in the existing system of the Colony can render it available to the purpose of its original Institution. . . . Transportation to New South Wales is intended as a severe Punishment applied to various Crimes, and as such must be rendered an object of real Terror to all Classes of the Community.

Bathurst had been chewing this over for some time, and in 1817 had appealed to the Home Secretary (Lord Sidmouth) to know whether there was any prospect of a diminution in the number of transported criminals. "I cannot conceal from myself," he added, "that Transportation to New South Wales is becoming neither an object of Apprehension here nor the means of Reformation in the Settlement itself, and that the Settlement must be either placed upon a footing that shall render it possible to enforce, with respect to all the Convicts, strict Discipline, Regular Labour, and constant Superintendance, or the System of unlimited Transportation to New South Wales must be abandoned." And even when in 1822 he was comforting the returned Macquarie as graciously as possible, praising in the King's name his assiduity and integrity and crediting his administration with the colony's advance in agriculture, trade, and wealth of every kind, he must still hark back to his old theme: "If, as a place of Punishment, it has not answered all the purposes for which it was intended, this is certainly not owing to any deficiency of Zeal or Solicitude on your part."

The effect on Macquarie of the dispatch of 30 January, 1819, need not be enlarged on. His young kingdom of the southern seas was to be judged by a stranger from some West-Indian island, not on its merits, but as the gaol from which he had striven to differentiate it. Further, this judge from Trinidad was given authority to investigate all the complaints made by Marsden and other recalcitrants against the Governor himself, not sparing "any individual, however exalted in rank or sacred in character." The pro-emancipist policy, too, was to come under the microscope, though Bathurst pointedly referred to it as "sanctioned by the Prince Regent" and "approved by the Government at home."

And all this must be endured although, as far as Macquarie knew, not even the courtesy of an acknowledgment had been extended to his earnest request for relief from duty.

John Thomas Bigge, who arrived in New South Wales on 26 September, 1819, was an almost ideally bad choice for such work as lay before him there. He was a lawyer of thirteen years' standing who for three of them had been chief justice of Trinidad; there he had learnt that society was formed of three layers, the officials and wealthy planters, the "poor whites," and the negroes a little (but not much) below them. He had no experience of administration, and the compromises and tactfulnesses it involves; he believed sincerely in the universal validity of logic and of the strictly legal view of rights and duties. What was worse, he had been inoculated at the Colonial Office with Goulburn's prejudices against the Governor on whom he was to sit in judgment. Before he had been six months in Sydney, he unburdened himself to John Macarthur; "there is but one excuse to be offered for your Governor," he said, "which is his total incapacity — but that of course Government have long known."

Happily ignorant of this prejudice—which must go a long way towards disqualifying Bigge's judgment on any matter personal to him—Macquarie received him with the utmost courtesy and a strong desire to assist his inquiries. Within a month Bigge was protesting vehemently against the promotion of William Redfern, an emancipist, to the magistracy (a promotion promised long before Bigge reached the colony), not on general principles—for Bigge had sat on the bench with Lord — but because Redfern when a youth of nineteen had been transported for taking a small share in the mutiny at the Nore. Seventeen years of excellent work in the colonial hospitals, a free pardon from Governor

King, the unstinted praise of Foveaux and Macquarie, and the acceptance of his advice as a medical man by the British Government itself, could not in Bigge's mind outweigh that twenty-two-year-old offence. Macquarie persisted in the appointment, and Bigge scored one point against him. A second was scored early in 1820, when Bigge discovered that Macquarie had been collecting opinions on his administration from magistrates and chaplains—this seemed to the Special Commissioner something approaching *lèse-majesté*, and he angrily broke off all personal relations with the Governor until such opinions as had come in were sealed up and put safely out of harm's way. A nominal reconciliation preceded Bigge's departure for Tasmania, where he further irritated Macquarie by interfering with his arrangements about the northern port of that island—in this case Bigge was right, but that made no difference to the irritation. Altogether the Commission was the last straw; on 29 February, 1820, Macquarie repeated his still unanswered request to be let go, and in March 1821—about a month after Bigge had sailed for England—received Bathurst's acceptance of his resignation. "Your Lordship," he replied, "may rest well assured that, after the many indignities and mortifications I have experienced *for the last Eighteen Months*, the early arrival of my Successor here will be to me a source of sincere pleasure."

He had still nine months of office, but little heart to use them for anything of importance, especially with the Bigge Report hanging over his head. In April he founded Port Macquarie, a settlement intended to relieve Newcastle of the overplus of convicts, but soon found too fertile and full of amenities to be wasted on a gaol; Moreton Bay replaced it in that capacity, and the port became the first Australian canefields location. Among his last dispatches as Governor, sent in October, was one enclosing (with his strong backing) a petition from his favourite emancipists; they protested against the denial of civil rights imposed on them by a decision of the Court of King's Bench that free pardons granted in the colony had no effect on their status as citizens —in the eyes of the law they were convicts, outside society to their dying day,[1] unless the Governor's pardon was confirmed in London by a pardon "under the Great Seal." Incidentally they produced statistics that throw light on the social condition of Macquarie's domain, and are worth reprinting:

	Free Men	Emancipists
Number, adults	1,550	7,556
Number, children of	878	5,859
Acreage cultivated by	10,787	29,028
Acreage under pasture owned by	198,367	212,335
Houses owned by	300	1,200
Cattle owned by	28,582	42,900
Sheep owned by	87,391	174,179
Horses owned by	1,553	2,415
Pigs owned by	6,304	18,563
Total value of property owned by	£597,464	£1,123,600

(Convicts and the actual garrison are of course omitted from this table.)

This would seem a striking justification of Macquarie's emancipist policy—and, at the same time, a challenge to the British Government to make up its mind quickly about the colony's future status. As a terror-inspiring gaol it was obviously a failure; convicts who could reform had a far better chance in New South Wales than in the England of

[1] Bigge, it should be noted, supported their claim when he reached England, and an Act of 1823 included a clause giving the validity of pardons under the Great Seal to all pardons colonially issued up to that time.

those days. Bigge, who was no fool when he could escape from his personal prejudices, admitted that Macquarie's work in this direction could not be undone—other bogeys must be found for criminals, and New South Wales must henceforth be dealt with as a settlement of free or freed men, to be supplied with convict labour (as Virginia had been long before) by way of aiding them to open up the country. The method he favoured for this transformation was mainly borrowed from John Macarthur, who believed (as did Wakefield after him) that a bold peasantry was not to be compared to a haughty aristocracy. What was wanted, said Macarthur (and to a willing hearer), was "a body of really respectable settlers — Men of real Capital — not needy adventurers. They should have Estates of at least 10,000 Acres. . . . Such a body of Proprietors would in a few years become wealthy and with the support of Government powerful as an Aristocracy." The advice was taken; Macquarie's limit of one hundred acres was cancelled, his successor was ordered to make grants of anything up to four square miles, and to allow the occupation of much bigger blocks by sheep-owners. As has been already shown, in 1821 the average holding was fifteen acres, by 1827 it was more than forty-eight acres, without including the areas occupied but not sold. As for the experiment in aristocracy-making, it was destined to embitter the lives of two Governors— Brisbane and Darling — before it collapsed under the pressure of a rival scheme. Macarthur based his system on free grants to "respectable" people, Wakefield his on sales at high prices to rich people; all that either did was to destroy Macquarie's ideal of steady development by a mass of small farmers, and to strew over huge undigested areas of Australia a network of sheep-runs, at once unreliable as producers of wealth and ineffective as absorbers of labour.

This, however, exceeds the ambit of a biography of Macquarie. He was not to know how his plans would be manhandled. On 1 December, 1821, he handed over his charge to Sir Thomas Brisbane—who seems to have been waiting open-mouthed for it since 1816—and in February 1822 left Port Jackson for England. There he occupied himself with revising his ample diaries and completing an account of his long stewardship; and there he died, unrewarded but not unhonoured, on 1 July, 1824. On the 11th his body was taken with some pomp, attended by many Scottish nobles and gentry but not a single representative of the Government he had served, from Duke Street through St. James's Square, up Regent Street and by Park Crescent into the "new" (Euston) Road, and so to the Hermitage Dock in Wapping, and to a grave in the family burial-ground on Mull.

Macquarie's *Apologia*, addressed to Earl Bathurst on 27 July, 1822, is one of the most triumphant and yet pathetic documents in the historical records of Australia. Self-laudatory it is, but only so far as a statement of facts must reflect credit on the man responsible for them. It began with a description, in no way overdrawn, of New South Wales as Macquarie first saw it:

> I found the Colony barely emerging from infantile imbecility, and suffering from various privations and disabilities; the Country impenetrable beyond 40 miles from Sydney; Agriculture in a yet languishing state; commerce in its early dawn; Revenue unknown; threatened by famine; distracted by faction; the public buildings in a state of dilapidation and mouldering to decay; the few Roads and Bridges, formerly constructed, rendered almost impassable; the population in general depressed by poverty; no public credit nor private confidence; the morals of the great mass of the population in the lowest state of debasement, and religious worship almost totally neglected.

Then, one by one, he enumerated his measures of reform. Precautions against famine came first, including those against the Hawkesbury floods. Then—a specially Macquarie-ish touch—reform of the public morals, partly preaching temperance, "diligent attendance at Divine Worship on Sundays, and that Marriage should take place of and supersede the disgraceful and immoral state of Concubinage, which I found generally prevailing on my arrival in the Colony"; partly by the establishment of schools all over the settled districts; partly by the encouragement of such emancipists as had "sustained unblemished characters since their emancipation. . . . I considered this as the first step towards a general reformation of the manners and habits of the motley part of the population." Next came his public-works policy, and agricultural, commercial and financial statistics that justified it by results; his treatment of the aborigines, of orphan children (of this he was always particularly proud), of the aged and infirm, of the convicts; his prevention of monopolies and high food-prices by the use of the Government herds and flocks, his final claim "that the Colony has under my orders and regulations greatly improved in agriculture, trade, increase of Flocks and Herds and wealth of every kind; that the People build better Dwelling houses and live more comfortably; that they are in a very considerable degree reformed in their moral and religious habits; that they are now less prone to Drunkenness, and more industrious; and that crimes have decreased, making due allowance for the late increase of Convict population." To all which, as we have seen, Bathurst's cold reply was that the improvement was highly creditable, but the colony was not meant to be improved; it should have been made a bogey to criminals, not a reformatory for penitents.

Lachlan Macquarie

Out of all this turmoil of administrative work and suffering —this almost feverish constructive activity, beset with the intrigues of surrounding officialdom, the recriminations of his nearest subordinates, the ingratitude of his subjects, the approval only of one distant master and of a few friends whose very friendship brought him ill-luck—what picture do we form of the man himself? He, no doubt, would have preferred to await posterity's verdict on his work alone; no man better deserved the epitaph that Wren won. But personality counts, as well as achievement, and the few personal touches we can gather from contemporary records deserve collation; his own voluminous diaries, preserved in the Mitchell Library at Sydney but not yet thoroughly studied, will some day help to complete the picture. Two portraits of him exist—one by Opie, depicting a grave, high-browed, Roman-nosed and rather narrow face, the face of a leader whose troops trust and admire but scarcely adore him; he could be kindly, but not often. The other, painted by the local artist, Robert Read senior, through all its crudities shows a more human, less reticently absorbed figure, fatherly for all its stubbornness and very, very weary. Hung near each other in the Dixson wing of the Public Library of New South Wales, they indicate what the colony did for the man who did so much for it. One remembers, too, that in his life Macquarie married twice. His first wife gave him in India three years of unalloyed happiness, a pattern for all marriages; he mourned her for nine years, and loved her to the day of his death. His second wife, met in Scotland during his leave of 1803–5, was the ideal wife for a Governor; her name is still commemorated (though far too little remembered) on the rocks of Port Jackson, and her work among the women and children of the settlement, white and aboriginal, was as valuable in its way as her husband's in his. Two such wives do not fall to the lot of an everyday mortal; the man who won both and kept them happy had exceptional personal charm—when he chose to use it. Outsiders' impressions of him were not always favourable; he was inclined to be "set in his judgments," as a man will be who has unwonted problems to encounter and no reliable advisers to help him; he was masterful withal, and straight-speaking, and slow to understand that unqualified rebukes, however well deserved, hurt subordinates who are doing their best without much praise (yet he felt the hurt personally when Bathurst spoke straight to him). When he had time, and was not too tired, and things were going well, he could unbend and enjoy a joke against himself; such moments were fewer as the burden of his isolated and misappreciated rule weighed him down.

Misappreciated, I say; depreciated, slandered, vilified, would be truer words. If Macquarie has been undervalued, and often denounced as a dull tyrant, it is because in his attempts to carry out vast schemes with insufficient and unsuitable material he fell foul of three bitter and narrow men. No man could incur unscathed the enmity of Samuel Marsden, Jeffery Bent, and John Thomas Bigge, and their reports of him were for many years accepted as correct. The man they depict could not have done the work Macquarie did. Nor could he have won the praise of Bathurst, the commendations of Macarthur (no friendly witness) which have been quoted above, the ungrudging admiration of William Charles Wentworth. And this short record of his real work and worth may close fitly with two eulogies pronounced after his departure, when it was not officially popular to praise him. The one comes from a Frenchman who never saw him, but only knew the colony as he left it:

L'erreur de l'administration de M. Maquarie a pu être de chercher à donner un vaste essor à la colonie qu'il dirigeait, mais cette erreur est celle d'une âme généreuse, et son souvenir doit rester dans le cœur des colons reconnaissants.

(R. P. Lesson, *Voyage autour du Monde sur la Corvette La Coquille*, ii. 237.)

The other, from the *Sydney Gazette* obituary notice, is the more trustworthy because all official and outside influences at the moment tended to suggest a merely formal and unenthusiastic valedictory:

There never was the individual yet, that had the honour of treading Australia's shore, more eminently beloved than the late General Macquarie.

WILLIAM CHARLES WENTWORTH

At Portadown in northern Ireland in the year 1762 was born D'Arcy Wentworth, one of the most intriguing characters in early Australian history. At the age of twenty he was ensign in the local volunteer regiment; three years later, the regiment being disbanded, he went off to London to study medicine. Two years after that, in November 1787, he was arrested at Notting Hill Gate—where, according to his landlady, he "behaved like a gentleman, and paid his way like a gentleman"—with a loaded pistol and a piece of black silk in his pocket, and in December stood his trial at the Old Bailey on two charges of having committed highway robbery on Hounslow Heath. Acquitted then, apparently for lack of satisfactory identification (a matter capable of friendly arrangement), he was quietly transferred by influential friends from London to Yorkshire; "considerable pains," said an indignant gentleman later on, "had been taken by myself and others to get him out of the kingdom." The speaker had in all probability reason for his indignation. He was a certain John Pemberton Heywood, who was ordered to stand and deliver at Finchley on 10 July, 1789, by someone "with a pretty strong Irish brogue," in consequence of which D'Arcy Wentworth was tried for the offence on 9 December. But his protection was too strong. Lord Fitzwilliam, a great Yorkshire Whig and a personal friend of the then Prince of Wales, was distantly connected with the Wentworths through Lord Rockingham, and was so proud of the connection that he afterwards obtained permission to alter his name to Fitzwilliam-

Wentworth. He could not let a genuine Wentworth go to the gallows. So Heywood was called off, the evidence was well watered down, and, the jury having done what was expected of it by acquitting him, the Crown Prosecutor (of all people!) announced in court that Mr. D'Arcy Wentworth had accepted an appointment as assistant surgeon in the fleet of convict transports that was about to sail for New Holland. He sailed accordingly in the *Neptune*, where he must have had many opportunities of becoming competent in his new profession, for the vessel lost during her outward voyage 158 convicts out of 502—mainly from scurvy and low fever; it is not suggested that Wentworth was in any way responsible, the behaviour of the master and crew to their unfortunate charges being quite bad enough to account for even a greater mortality rate. Phillip on his arrival allotted him to Norfolk Island, where he was assistant in the hospital for five years, gained the approval of Lieutenant-Governor King, and on 10 December, 1791, was made a superintendent of convicts—a position of trust. His subsequent career was entirely meritorious. In his profession he rose to be principal surgeon of New South Wales (under Macquarie); outside it he was favoured by Governor after Governor, granted large areas of land (large for those days) because he used so well what was given him, made (also by Macquarie) head of the Sydney police force and a magistrate, and died at sixty-five a well-respected and much-valued citizen.

Where, then, lies the puzzle? Mainly in the man's early reputation and doings. Though he had been acquitted in 1789 and went out to Australia a free man, he was always regarded by officials as having been originally transported. In London they classed him with George Barrington, and the publisher of the alleged Barrington *Voyage to New South*

Wales and *History of New South Wales* ascribed to him, as a personal friend of George's, all the information that could be scraped together about Norfolk Island in the first years of the nineteenth century. Even the sober *Annual Register* in 1792 mentioned "Wentworth, the highwayman," as medical officer at Norfolk Island, adding that he "behaves himself remarkably well. He is also tutor to the children of the colony." Macquarie himself, it is to be feared, was all the more eager to promote him because he was thought to be a striking example of what an emancipist could rise to.

Again—and this is particularly relevant to our real subject—his family life on Norfolk Island has never been clearly understood. His wife's name was Catherine, and she is usually identified with the Catherine Parry who was emancipated at Norfolk Island in or before October 1791 "on her marrying a superintendent." Her eldest son's birth is in this story dated 26 October, 1793. Unfortunately (*a*) D'Arcy was not made a superintendent until December 1791; (*b*) the only man capable of performing marriages, Richard Johnson, the colonial chaplain, did not visit Norfolk Island until 4 November in that year; (*c*) if young Wentworth was born in 1793, then Macquarie made him acting Provost-Marshal of New South Wales on his eighteenth birthday, and within a month of it he was entering into a bond to pay £168. Strange things happened at times in early New South Wales; but under Macquarie, and just when he was clearing up the mess left behind by the Bligh mutiny . . . no! The truth probably is that on the outward voyage D'Arcy Wentworth contracted with a convict girl one of those irregular alliances that were very general under such conditions; that he was allowed to take her with him to Norfolk Island, where William Charles was born towards the end of 1790 (an unpublished Life of him, probably on the authority of Sir James Martin, gives that date in MS.); and that, the alliance being irregular only from force of circumstances, William's parents were married by Richard Johnson at the earliest opportunity, and their subsequent life was normally and respectably happy.

All this may seem an unnecessary raking up of bygone scandals. It is, however, of considerable importance in the explanation of William's own life. His younger brothers, born in less exciting circumstances, had no trace of his genius, his driving-power, or his astonishing recklessness at the wrong time. One entered the army, was the first Australian-born recipient of His Majesty's commission as an officer, and after a respectable but undistinguished military career retired on half-pay in 1843, and died in Tasmania in 1861. Another joined the navy, and was drowned off the coast of Africa in 1829. William alone, true son of the "highwayman," with his father's dare-devilishness fully developed and his father's ability raised to the nth power, managed to combine a clear-headed vigour in attack that was often statesmanlike with a fantastic carelessness about details that laid him open to dangerous ripostes—so that the man who freed the Australian press and fashioned the type-form of colonial constitutions also became the most notorious of New Zealand land-grabbers and the father of ridiculous proposals for an Australian House of Lords.

At the earliest possible age—when he was certainly six years old and probably nine—William Charles was sent off to England to be put to school at Greenwich. His father intended him for a soldier, but all the Fitzwilliam influence failed to gain him admission to the military academy. In 1811 it became clear that the family was permanently settled in Sydney, and William rejoined them there, full of youthful ardour and inexperience. Governor Macquarie, anxious to please D'Arcy Wentworth, appointed the boy acting Provost-Marshal — a sufficiently responsible post for a lad of twenty-one—and he started life for himself with six cows on a small farm forty miles inland from Sydney. There he made the acquaintance of Gregory Blaxland, whose life is dealt with later in this volume; and when, in 1813, Blaxland and Lawson organised their expedition into the Blue Mountains, young Wentworth eagerly joined them and set his name on the roll of Australian explorers. (His journal of the adventure, as might be expected, is the least informative, the most excited of the three.) A year later he was off again, this time joining a schooner in search of sandalwood in the South Sea Islands; at Rarotonga in the Cook group he was all but killed by hostile natives, and when the master of the vessel died on the voyage he used what mathematical knowledge he had acquired at school to bring her back to Sydney. In 1816, no more local adventures offering, he asked his father to let him go back to England, and, when his passage was secured, burst into an orgy of lampooning. In these "pipes," as they were locally called, William did not spare his own father, whom he dubbed "the Count" and accused of gluttony and favouritism; but the worst of them were aimed at Colonel Molle, then in command of the garrison, who had quarrelled with D'Arcy Wentworth—believing, no doubt, that he was an emancipist—and had by overmuch boasting of his own military record laid himself open to retorts. William was safe at sea before the "pipes" appeared, and they were for a time attributed to his father; Molle's junior officers [1]

---

[1] The bitter feeling between ex-convicts and the military may be judged from the language used by these officers:
"These [the 'pipes'] we perceive issuing from the Pen of Men so much Our Inferiors in Rank and Situation, that We know them

backed him with vehemence, incidentally sneering at Macquarie's hospitality to the better class of emancipist, and the irate Governor was within an ace of having the colonel court-martialled. The discovery of the true culprit's identity and the ample apology made on his behalf by D'Arcy Wentworth allowed the affair to be smoothed over. Its real importance was that it labelled both the Wentworths as champions of the growing emancipist section, and gave William Charles, when later on he returned to Sydney, a definite standing with an important class of colonists.

England, which the boy reached at the end of 1816, was at first no more exciting than Sydney had been. D'Arcy had hoped that his son would join the army, but Waterloo put an end to that kind of excitement, and young Wentworth decided to study for the Bar, entering at the Middle Temple on 5 February, 1817. Still restless, in April he petitioned the Colonial Office for leave to go back to Australia and devote himself to exploring it from east to west; that forbidden, he travelled for a while in Europe, but ill-health (he was threatened with tuberculosis, the doctors said) and the miseries he encountered in lands not yet recovered from the Napoleonic wars drove him back to London. There, to savour his legal studies, he set himself to write and publish the first book on the Australian colonies that came from the pen of a native. *A Statistical, Historical, and Political Description of the Colony of New South Wales*, published in 1819, was not only what its title claimed for it, but also a reasoned appeal for more self-government and more settlers. A second edition was called for in 1820, a third in 1824, and

not but among that promiscuous Class, which (with Pride We speak it) have been ever excluded from intercourse with *Us*."

The italics are in the original. The subaltern of those days had a fine talent, obviously, for contumelious language.

no less an authority than Edward Gibbon Wakefield considered that it had stimulated emigration to a remarkable degree.

On 8 February, 1822, William was called to the Bar. His intention was to practise in Australia; as he was not yet inclined to return there, he filled in time by procuring admission as a fellow-commoner of Peterhouse at Cambridge, but there is no record at the university of his having matriculated. This did not prevent him from giving his beloved country further advertisement by competing in 1823 for the Chancellor's medal for English poetry.[1] The subject was "Australasia"; and the young poet poured into the classical mould required for academic verse such enthusiasm as may have set his pulses tingling when in 1813, at the side of Lawson and Blaxland, he had viewed the "mighty ridge" of the Blue Mountains:

> How mute, how desolate, thy stunted woods,
> How dread thy chasms, where many an eagle broods,
> How dark thy caves, how lone thy torrents' roar
> As down thy cliffs precipitous they pour
> Broke on our hearts, when first with venturous tread
> We dared to rouse thee from thy mountain bed!
> Till, gained with toilsome step thy rocky heath,
> We spied the cheering smokes ascend beneath.
> Till, nearer seen, the beauteous landscape grew,
> Opening like Canaan on rapt Israel's view.

W. M. Praed's poem, which was placed first, was doubtless more scrupulously in accord with the academic type of verse then in fashion, but was ludicrously disfigured by his ignorance of his subject. He waxed pathetic in very saccharine

[1] The poem was written within three weeks, and a cryptic note to the published version says that he would have much emended it "had he joined the university a month sooner."

laments over the convict transports, and drew a picture of New South Wales that would do credit to an immigration agent:

> Therefore on thee undying sunbeams throw
> Their clearest radiance, and their warmest glow,
> And tranquil nights, cool gales, and gentle showers
> Make bloom eternal in thy sinless bowers.

Then he peopled this Eden with dying Maori chiefs, whose widows stained their eyebrows with burnt emu-feathers. Wentworth's Australia was at any rate real, however stilted the language in which he had to describe it; his aborigines, his farmlands along the Parramatta and Nepean, his busy Sydney, sheltered then by forests from the violence of the "southerly buster," his South Sea traders and his whalers, all were true to life. What possibly cost him the prize—for even dons then were patriotic—was his final prophecy that, when Britain,

> no longer freest of the free,
> To some proud victor bend'st the vanquished knee,

then her great traditions might create a successor in the far-away Pacific,

> And Australasia float, with flag unfurled,
> A new Britannia in another world!

It was, after all, a rather magnificent piece of braggadocio —especially when addressed to the Britannia of those days, invincible ruler of the waves and in some sort arbiter of Europe—and it might easily lose him the Chancellor's medal, though it roused admirers to demand that the poem should be published for the world's benefit. Before the end of the year, therefore, *Australasia, A Poem written for the Chancellor's Medal at the Cambridge Commencement,* 1823, appeared in pamphlet form with a dedication to Governor Lachlan Macquarie.

Wentworth's book had in 1819 gained him the close friendship of Robert Wardell, a barrister who was at the time editing a London evening newspaper, the *Statesman*. When in 1823 rumours were current that, as a result of Bigge's report and the new Constitution Act, censorship of the press might soon cease to exist in New South Wales, the friends decided to adventure in Australian journalism; Wardell sold his interest in the *Statesman* for £3000, bought with the money the necessary type and paper, and in July 1824 reached Sydney with Wentworth. Their notion was that, while Wardell devoted his main attention to journalism, Wentworth should practise assiduously at the Bar, the efforts of both being directed towards (*a*) championship of the emancipists and the less influential free settlers; (*b*) advocacy by all methods of a free press, trial by jury, and much enlarged powers of self-government. Wentworth's book had long since laid down the bases on which they proposed to build. Always a strong supporter of Macquarie's ideals, and a steady antagonist of Bigge (whom he described as "a booby commissioner," coupling him with the "madman" Barron Field and the "crafty priest" Samuel Marsden), he saw in the emancipist community a breed capable of rich developments: "Whatever the private morals and failings of these people may be—and the greater number of them are not worse in this respect than their unconvicted fellow-colonists—they have been politically, and, as far as human laws are concerned, morally reformed." As for immigrants, Australian opportunities would work on them just as marvellous a change; labourers would soon find themselves well off, tenant farmers would become independent landed proprietors, artisans would develop into manufacturers on a large scale. Nor did he think that the influx of free settlers need interfere with the continued use of the colony as a convict station; convicts, he said, were "a great body of labourers at the disposal of the Government; and the great object, so to employ them as to make the employment penal and reformatory to them, and as useful and inexpensive as possible to the State." Therefore the type of settler needed was one with capital and enterprise who would employ convicts in large numbers; and convicts retained in the Government service should be mainly used to clear and prepare farms for such settlers.

In September 1824 the friends were admitted barristers of the Supreme Court, and one of Wentworth's first cases concerned an unsuccessful attempt to place the names of emancipists on the colony's jury lists. Wardell's initial venture was made on 14 October, when the first issue of the *Australian* appeared without official permission or censorship. Governor Brisbane, who quietly favoured the freedom of the press, felt himself bound to consult his legal adviser on this innovation, and welcomed the discovery that under the new Charter of Justice (which had been promulgated in the previous May) proceedings could not be taken against the editors without putting the matter before the Legislative Council. It was in fact probable that the Council as then constituted would have supported censorship, and Brisbane determined to evade this by withdrawing it on his own responsibility—a step which he never regretted. For a year or two the young men lived in an atmosphere of kindly approval, Francis Forbes (the new Chief Justice) describing them to the Colonial Office as "gentlemen of very respectable legal talents and knowledge, but a little inclining against the powers that be," and Brisbane's successor, Darling, regarding the *Australian* with special favour, and vehemently asserting the merits of Wardell against the criticisms of his own legal adviser, Saxe Bannister.

But behind the general kindliness the old class warfare still lay dormant. The official cliques, the older landowners, especially the military officers who had settled down to be, as they believed, a dominant and exclusive aristocracy, watched with jealous eyes every movement towards equalising the status or enlarging the liberties of men outside their own narrow circles. In 1820 Barron Field had warned Bigge:

> I see the shadow of the spirit of American revolt at taxation, rising in the shape of a petition for trial by jury; it will next demand legislative assembly; and end in declaring itself a nation of freebooters and pirates.

Many otherwise sober citizens shared that nightmare with him, and looked on Wentworth and Wardell as precursors and inspirers of an Australian Revolution. As long, however, as they retained Government House favour, nothing could be done. But towards the end of 1826, just when money was "tight" and trade bad throughout the colony, Darling tried to stop malingering soldiers from deliberately committing crimes in order to become convicts (they thought the prisoners were better looked after than the garrison) by inflicting severe punishment on two such offenders. For the times the punishment was not over-brutal, but one of the victims died a few days after enduring it. At once Wentworth—who had never fully reciprocated Darling's friendliness—burst into violent invective, demanded the Governor's recall, and based on the affair a whirlwind campaign for the extension of full citizen rights to all non-prisoners, and the creation of an elected legislative assembly. Darling's only weapon against this attack was an attempt to restore press censorship by imposing heavy stamp duties on newspapers and insisting on a licence; these were not his own measures, but had been recommended to him before he left England by officials who doubted the wisdom of Brisbane's generous concession. The Chief Justice—who, under the sometimes fantastic provisions of the Charter of Justice had to certify in advance that proposed laws were not repugnant to the existing English law—held that the duties and the licence would illegally limit a Briton's natural right to free speech. Nothing was left to Darling but to prosecute his opponents for seditious libel, and by 1829 the trial of such actions occupied nearly the whole time of the Supreme Court. The only lasting result was to increase remarkably Wentworth's reputation as an advocate (for he was the obvious and inevitable counsel for the defence) and to strengthen the case against the system of military jurors which still obtained in New South Wales. In 1830 trial by jury in the true English sense of the word was established in the colony, and Wentworth's first real victory was won. To emphasise it he turned the Governor's weapon against his own side, successfully prosecuted the *Gazette*—Darling's organ—for reporting a bitter attack made on his personal character by Darling himself, and finally, in 1831, secured the Governor's recall.[1] The whole episode is sometimes treated as a great constitutional victory over a blindly blundering autocrat; but in truth, though neither of the protagonists comes out of it laudably, yet Darling was the cleaner-handed of the two. He was a martinet, no doubt,

[1] In 1835 a Parliamentary Committee was appointed to investigate the charges made against Governor Darling by Wentworth and others. On the charge of brutality to convicted soldiers the Governor was held innocent, no other charges were proceeded with, and in 1836 the long-suffering man was knighted.

tactless, and towards the end personally exasperated, but he was to the best of his ability doing his duty as representative of the British Government and obeying orders given him from London. Wentworth, with far greater abilities, was far more unscrupulous; he deliberately used every means, fair or foul, to gain his ends and crush his opponent; his aims were high enough and, on the whole, disinterested, but his temperamental vindictiveness thought every method of attaining them excusable, and betrayed him into almost indecent exultation when Darling left the colony.

With that departure his first objectives—freedom of the press, trial by citizen juries, and equalisation of the emancipists' status — were practically won. During Governor Bourke's term of office he devoted himself to advocating a freer form of government and—sad fall from his earlier altruism—fuller local control of the colony's unoccupied territories. The campaign for really representative government had begun in 1827, when a petition for a legislature of one hundred members (to be elected on manhood suffrage) was presented to the British Parliament, but scornfully shelved by the Colonial Office as mere emancipist bluff. In 1833, however, Wentworth's following was swelled by the accession of a large number of free settlers who had reached the colony during the twenties, but had prudently kept out of politics while the campaign of libel trials was going on. Further, to his special sympathiser at Westminster, the Radical Joseph Hume, were now added several members of the influential clique at whose centre was Edward Gibbon Wakefield, besides the somewhat incongruous figure of Henry Lytton Bulwer. In the colony Wardell (who had refused to follow his friend into extremes of vindictiveness against Darling) had been murdered by convicts in 1834, but his place was taken by William Bland—an able dis-

William Charles Wentworth

putant and a friend of the family since 1814—and a triumvirate was formed by the accession of John Jamison, leader of the young free settlers. During the thirties these three carried on a persistent campaign for an elected legislature; in May 1837 they created the Australian Patriotic Association, and soon afterwards thoughtfully supplied the Colonial Office with alternative drafts of a constitution—one providing a single House of fifty members, forty elected on a much-restricted franchise; the other allowing all the fifty to be elected but adding a second House of fifteen nominees. Charles Buller, Wakefield's friend, was appointed the Association's agent at Westminster and instructed to press the first scheme, which after some years of negotiation —the delay being due chiefly to the need of first abolishing transportation—was adopted in a much-modified shape by an Act of 1842. The qualification of voters was still further narrowed, and the proportion of nominees was increased to twelve out of a total of thirty-six; but at last there was genuine representation, and it was undoubtedly Wentworth's efforts—more praiseworthy and more effective when free from all trace of malevolence—that were responsible for the result.

Of Wentworth's private life during these years—as of the privacy of most Australians, who have never learnt to believe that their homes and their friendships should be shared with the press or the public—there is little record except what may be inferred from the walls that sheltered it. His house at Vaucluse, well within the entering curve of Port Jackson and commanding the harbour northwards to Manly and westwards towards Sydney, now stands in a public park and is maintained as an historical museum. It had a history before Wentworth owned it; an earlier owner was Henry Brown Hayes, Irishman, abductor of a fair

Quakeress, founder of the first Masonic lodge in Australia, and perpetual thorn in the side of Governor King. Hayes bought Vaucluse in 1803, imported tons of soil from Ireland to keep the snakes out (the bill of lading was quite recently in existence), and leased the property next year. Presently it came into the hands of John Piper, racing man and one of the best of early Australian "good fellows," who made it for fourteen lively years the week-end rendezvous of sportsmen. In 1827 he sold it to Wentworth, who—it is pleasant to record—found he had acquired the estate too cheaply, and insisted on paying Piper several thousand pounds more to make the bargain fair. From that time the week-ends became more sober, and the mansion was dedicated to more statesmanlike uses; for in the spacious library were devised not only campaigns for political freedom and attacks on hated Governors and negotiations with Opposition leaders, but the famous draft of a constitution which in 1855 the Colonial Office accepted as the pattern for Australian freedom.

The comparatively peaceful years ended in 1840. Governor Bourke, who valued and almost consistently followed Wentworth's advice, was in 1838 succeeded by Governor Gipps, a man in whom Darling's martinet qualities and devotion to duty were magnified and transformed by abilities scarcely if at all below Macquarie's. He began with a readiness to accept Wentworth on Bourke's terms, and heartily supported in principle his demands for a representative legislature. But at a critical moment Wentworth's altruism — his most effective political asset — broke down, and Gipps never trusted him again. His association with Jamison's followers, and his growing wealth, attracted him irresistibly to the land-owning and stock-raising clique whose members — in the old days of oppressed emancipism—had been his hated foes. In 1836 he abandoned legal work to give more attention to his pastoral properties, and began to adapt his political convictions to the interests of the squatting fraternity, demanding cheap land for their flocks to graze on, cheap labour—either of convicts or of imported coolies—for their station work, and a restricted franchise (no more of the 1827 manhood suffrage) to make them dominant in politics. In most of these matters, however, Bourke and Gipps successfully withstood him; he accepted the defeat, and turned to New Zealand, just then the theatre of the astounding Wakefield land-grabbing exploits, to acquire the vast areas he needed for his pastoral schemes. In 1840 a few petty Maori chiefs visited Sydney, and Gipps found himself thwarted in his negotiations with them by some hidden influence. Inquiries disclosed that Wentworth was simultaneously warning them against the acceptance of British suzerainty, and buying from them for "a farthing a hundred acres," according to Gipps, no less than twenty million acres of pasture-land in what is now the province of Canterbury. From the moment of that discovery Gipps and Wentworth were implacable enemies. It was Australia's great misfortune that two such able leaders, at so critical a time in the development of her institutions, found co-operation impossible. All Wentworth's advocacy of needed reforms was thenceforth tainted with a virulence and a vindictiveness more deplorable than he had displayed against Darling. All Gipps's eagerness to obtain those reforms from the Colonial Office was sicklied o'er with the persistent suspicion that anything backed by this unscrupulous antagonist must be dangerous. Gipps himself was in a most unenviable position, full of intelligent sympathy for the colonists but bound as Governor to carry out the policy dictated to him from Downing Street. In London his advocacy of concessions was weakened by his known dislike of the leader who demanded them;

in Sydney he was continually misrepresented as the author or progenitor of measures in whose administration he was actually a very unwilling instrument.

So much said, we may proceed to consider the story of the 1840's without further reference to any personal quarrels. The long-desired representative Council was established in 1843, Wentworth and Bland joining it as members for Sydney; Jamison was already too ill to stand for election, and died in the following year. One of Wentworth's first achievements in the Council was to pass a Bill, of great importance to the pastoral industry then and ever since, under which wool could be mortgaged on the sheep's back, and stock without delivery to the mortgagee. The Colonial Office, staggered at the innovation, disallowed the Bill, but without effect; it was replaced by temporary enactments of an identical character until Downing Street's opposition was worn down. In 1844 Wentworth, aggrieved by an increase in the fees payable for pasturage beyond the bounds of settlement, formed a Pastoral Association to defend the squatters' interests, and entered on a campaign to secure for the Council full control of land revenues, which the Constitution of 1842 had left in the Governor's personal control.[1] But this was merely one episode of his persistent fight for full citizen rights. The Constitution of 1842 left the Governor actual, not nominal, head of the executive; he could choose, and could maintain in office, ministers of whom the majority of the Council disapproved. Pastoralists,

---

[1] Half of them must be spent on assisting immigration; from the other half Gipps was empowered to finance measures for the welfare of the aborigines, the construction of roads and bridges outside the bounds of settlement, and the maintenance of a Border police force. Any surplus went into the Treasury, and so came under the Council's control.

however wealthy, had no vote as such; unless they owned sufficient property within the settled districts,[1] they were disfranchised. And besides the revenue from Crown lands, over £80,000 of annual expenditure (nearly a third of the total) was placed on a "Civil List" and so removed from the Council's control. These grievances, said Wentworth, did not exist in Canada:

> It is as if Great Britain should say, "You, Canada, have rebelled; you have mown down our troops, you have bayoneted and bulleted our soldiers. You, Australians, have been uniformly obedient, patient, submissive, and loyal. Therefore we will grant to Canada her territorial revenue and her waste lands; and in Australia we will impose a disproportionate Civil List without compensation."

But the Colonial Office during the 1840's was incurably doctrinaire, partly because its permanent officials resented the ingratitude of colonists who would not accept dutifully what they were given, partly because two of its ministerial heads were afflicted with that particular temperament. Lord Stanley, who had done his best to support Gipps against Downing Street whenever the two were in conflict, resigned in December 1845. William Ewart Gladstone, his immediate successor, promptly created an entirely new source of turmoil by proposing to re-establish transportation—under much ameliorated conditions, certainly, but still transportation (as we shall see, he had Wentworth's backing in this proposal). And Earl Grey, who administered the Colonial Office

[1] The "settled districts" consisted of an area stretching along the coast about 250 miles north of Sydney and about 175 miles south, and bounded inland by a shallow curve with a radius (roughly speaking) of about 170 miles from Sydney. Land outside these "bounds of location" could not be sold, but might be occupied by squatters holding a licence to depasture.

from 1846 to 1852, was a full-blown flower of Wakefield doctrinairism, convinced that his nostrums were panaceas, placidly contemplating a future when all colonies would be independent of Great Britain, but determined that, until that came about, they should take the medicines he had in his spoon for them. In July 1846, just after Grey's entry on office, Gipps was allowed to retire, utterly worn out; he died in February 1847. His successor, Sir Charles FitzRoy, was a man of wholly different temperament, who took little personal interest in colonial affairs; he was only too glad to leave the real work of administration to his official secretary, Edward Deas Thomson, who promptly established a *modus vivendi* with Wentworth and for the next eight years or so worked in harmony with him on most subjects.

This amounted to a temporary triumph for the squatting interests, which were granted fixity of tenure for their runs and the right to buy cheaply when the leases expired. But the triumph itself created a new situation, in which a new political party forced the issues and at times dominated Wentworth and Deas Thomson together. Gladstone, as we have seen, tried to re-establish transportation, and Wentworth, on the look out for cheap and abundant labour, reported to the Council in favour of the scheme. At once there was an uproar, and petitions streamed in from Sydney, Parramatta, Liverpool, the Hunter River district — the whole colony, that is, except the areas controlled by pastoralists. The malcontents soon found a leader—Robert Lowe (afterwards Lord Sherbrooke), who had entered the Council in 1843 as a nominee of Governor Gipps, had quarrelled with his nominator, resigned, reappeared in the Council as member for the southern coastal counties, and had since been the Ishmael of the legislature. At what seemed the acme of Wentworth's parliamentary triumph, when only four of the elected councillors were not squatters and the obnoxious Gipps was recalled, Lowe seized his chance to organise a popular revolt; all through 1847 he worked hard, and at the general election of 1848 challenged Wentworth and Bland in their stronghold of Sydney. Wentworth won through, mainly by reminding voters of his earlier career, but Bland succumbed, and Lowe, with his lieutenant Henry Parkes (of whom more anon), became a popular hero. Almost the last act of the expiring legislature had been to sanction an agreement with the Colonial Office whereby New South Wales should accept as immigrants equal numbers of free settlers and ticket-of-leave men. In June 1849 the first consignment arrived, Downing Street, with its usual lack of tact, having omitted to include any free men in it; the *Hashemy* in Port Jackson and the *Randolph* in Hobson's Bay were met with stormy assemblages and threats of riot and mutterings about Boston tea-parties and revolution. Wentworth blustered, and had the Governor's personal feelings on his side. But FitzRoy was a natural pacificist; why, he thought, risk insurrection in Sydney when behind Moreton Bay (Brisbane) an almost isolated colony of pastoralists was clamouring for cheap labour? The detested vessels moved northwards unobtrusively. By 1850 Lowe and his new party had the Council under their thumb, and a strong Anti-Transportation League mastered all the larger centres of population from Sydney south to Hobart. The Colonial Office, where Grey fought to the last for his pet theories, collapsed when in February 1852 he left it; the news of gold discoveries, and the certainty that they would bring about an immense influx of free and rather undisciplined immigrants, showed up the folly of its obstinacy about convicts; in June the new Secretary, Sir John Pakington, announced that transportation to eastern Australia would be definitely abandoned before the end of the year. This was the one great reform of his period in which Wentworth had no share, and his opposition to it was emphasised in the public mind when men heard that, defeated over convict labour, he was in 1852 attempting to import coolies from India.

If one is inclined to wonder that the great advocate of local control and colonial freedom found himself in this crisis so utterly at variance with the mass of his fellow-countrymen, Henry Parkes supplies the answer:

> He was saturated with Lord Durham's report on the constitutional grievances of Canada, and stimulated to activity by his intercourse with liberal-minded men in England; and there is no ground for doubting his sincerity in espousing the cause of the people. But it may be, with just reason, doubted whether "The People" ever in his mind included the masses of his fellow-men.

"I was never a Radical, but always a Whig," said Wentworth himself, but that hardly expresses the truth. He was from first to last a hater of officialdom and official privileges, a believer in intellect and in the right of active intellect to rule. He fought for the emancipists because he was convinced that on the whole they were abler and more efficient citizens than the soldiers and officials of the "exclusive" clique. When he discovered among the young capitalist-immigrants of the 1820's—John Jamison's followers — men as able and efficient in the development of the land he loved (I mean that phrase), he took them to his heart, identified them with his favourite emancipists, and invented for their and his opponents—who had previously been known as "free settlers" or "old settlers"—the nickname "exclusionists." Never adopted by any official authority, the name yet gained currency and was a valuable weapon in his fight against Darling and the Colonial Office; no new arrival, unless he already had ties binding him to the official and military clique, was likely to let himself be labelled "exclusionist" or "exclusive."

Once entangled with Jamison's friends and entrusted with some governmental responsibility, Wentworth easily persuaded himself that his country was safer and more ably ruled by squatters than by small traders and townsfolk. Whether this belief and its resulting actions swelled or diminished his popularity he cared not a jot. He would lead the people if they would follow him; if not, he would go his own way, and they might go theirs at their own risk. But he firmly believed that they would follow him if they thought things out; the problem was how to train the masses (and the "classes," too, for that matter) to think. That threw him into the business of providing a sound education for young Australians of every class; and that flung him for a short time into the arms of Robert Lowe.

In 1844 a Parliamentary Committee demanded by Lowe had discovered that half the population between the ages of four and fourteen was receiving no education at all. What schools there were were under denominational control, and it took Lowe and Wentworth four years' hard fighting to establish a system of primary non-denominational schools side by side with the others. By 1850 the 185 subsidised schools belonging to the Anglican, Presbyterian, Roman Catholic and Wesleyan churches had been supplemented with 95 schools under a non-denominational board; from this beginning, it may fairly be said, sprang the primary-school system of to-day, which Henry Parkes built up in two great Acts (of 1867 and 1880) on his greater antagonist's foundations. It is not, however, as the founder of Australia's primary education that Wentworth is remembered; those foundations are buried too deep. His enduring monument in this regard is the University of Sydney.

The young squatter immigrants of the early twenties had made several attempts to create for their growing families a local school very roughly approximating to the Harrow or Rugby type. In 1825 such a "grammar school" came into being, but soon died. In 1835 it was revived as "The Sydney College," and maintained a precarious existence for twelve years, starved by its trustees as to teachers' salaries but provided with fine buildings. In 1847 the school collapsed again, the buildings fell vacant, and Wentworth saw his chance. Higher education was not specially popular just then, and Wentworth himself was, as we have seen, specially unpopular; but by 1849 he had persuaded the trustees to part with their property and (with Lowe's help) the Council to appoint a really strong committee, which in September reported in favour of the immediate foundation,

upon a liberal and comprehensive basis, of a University which shall be accessible to all classes and to all collegiate and affiliated institutions which shall seek its affiliation.

In 1850 the University Act was passed, after some disputes about the composition of the first senate; Wentworth included in his list the name of his friend William Bland, who was chairman of trustees of the Sydney College, but Lowe—never able to work whole-heartedly with any equal—refused to consider the inclusion of an ex-convict, and Wentworth was forced to sacrifice his friend to his university. The Sydney College buildings were found to be altogether inadequate,[1] a block of land on the edge of the city was handed

[1] In 1856 they were surrendered by the university and used to house a revived school, which as "The Sydney Grammar School" occupies them to this day.

over by the Government, and with three professors and twenty-four undergraduates the university was inaugurated in October 1852. Wentworth, who had conceived and created it, is still indisputably its hero; and the vagaries of his political career, his "Whiggism" and his undemocratic struggles against a wide franchise and popular power, are forgotten or forgiven for the nobly democratic achievement whereby he hoped to make every citizen fit for the highest responsibilities. "So far," he said in advocating the Bill of 1850, "from this being an institution for the rich, I take it to be an institution for the poor. . . . It opens the path to every child in the colony to greatness and usefulness in the destinies of his country. . . . I see in this measure the unerring figure which points out to the poor man's child the road to all that is respectable in position, all that is lofty and dignified in the estimation of his fellow-countrymen." Whether his successors have maintained the ideals of their founder is a question that need not be discussed here.

Before the university had actually taken shape, Wentworth was busy with the last great campaign of his life. The doctrinairism of the Colonial Office flowered most brilliantly in Earl Grey's 1847 scheme for a bicameral legislature of which the Assembly should be elected indirectly through district councils. That defeated (mainly through Wentworth's concentration of the popular hatred in a magnificent denunciation), a substitute provided in 1850 remedied a few colonial grievances (e.g. by separating Port Phillip under the name of Victoria and by widening the franchise), but retained the independence of the executive and the Governor's control over part of the revenue. Luckily it included a provision allowing the local legislature to suggest amendments in its own constitution. Wentworth seized the opportunity, in 1851 persuaded the Council to draw up a

Declaration and Remonstrance, and in 1852 secured the creation of a Parliamentary Committee which should devise for New South Wales its own constitution. The Declaration is a document of such vigour and importance—Parkes called it "one of the foundation-stones of the fabric of our constitutional liberties"—that it needs notice here, both for that reason and for the light it throws on the aims and beliefs of its author. It arraigns the Colonial Office for neglecting or intensifying every grievance of which New South Wales had been complaining for ten years, for clinging to "the exploded fallacies of the Wakefield theory" and so checking the flow of immigration:

> The bestowal of office among us, with but partial exception, is still exercised by or at the nomination of the Colonial Minister . . . as if the Colony itself were but the fief of that Minister. . . . All the material powers exercised for centuries by the House of Commons are still withheld from us; our loyalty and desire for the maintenance of order and good government are so far distrusted that we are not permitted to vote our own Civil List . . . our Waste Lands, and our Territorial Revenue, for which Her Majesty is but a Trustee, instead of being spontaneously surrendered as the equivalent for such Civil List, is still reserved, to the great detriment of all classes of Her Majesty's subjects, in order to swell the patronage and power of the Ministers of the Crown.

The "Declaration, Protest, and Remonstrance" (Wentworth was determined that there should be no mistake about its nature) concluded with five definite demands, which may be thus condensed:

> All powers of taxation, and the control of all revenues derived from land or customs, must be left solely to the local legislature;
> "Offices of trust and emolument should be conferred only on the settled inhabitants, the office of Governor alone excepted";
> The Governor must be appointed, and paid by, the Crown;
> Local patronage must be left in the hands of the Governor and Executive Council, unfettered by the Colonial Office;

The local legislature must have full legislative powers, no Bills being reserved "for the signification of Her Majesty's pleasure, unless they affect the Prerogatives of the Crown or the general interests of the Empire."

This whole-souled defiance of Grey's creed and practice was met by him with unmitigated stubbornness. But his successor, John Pakington, softening the blow to Grey's amour-propre with a reference to the gold discoveries, yielded gracefully, and even suggested that Wentworth and his friends should frame their own constitution. Within a month he, too, was out of office, but the Duke of Newcastle, who followed him, lost no time in announcing:

I have always thought it probable that the experience and wisdom of the Council would dictate better provisions than Parliament for securing good government in New South Wales;

and Wentworth's Committee of 1852, which was of his own devising, found itself converted into an authorised instrument of Imperial policy. On 9 August, 1853, he brought the Committee's (i.e. his own) report before the Council in the shape of a Bill.

Nothing is more characteristic of the man, in all his strength and his weaknesses, than his conduct of this last great political campaign. Fully aware of the wasps' nest he was stirring up, he introduced into the Bill proposals for an hereditary Australian peerage, the first peers having a seat for life in the Upper House of the legislature and their heirs a right to choose a certain number of representatives in that House. By way of conciliating opposition to so astounding a scheme he took occasion on the second reading of the Bill to attack both the Sydney merchants—

They as a class, with the exception of the ship-owners, are productive of absolutely nothing to add to the real wealth of the colony. There is no urgent necessity for them—the colony could do without them—

and the rising tide of democracy:

> Who would stay here if he could avoid it? Who with ample means would ever return if once he left these shores, or even identify himself with the soil so long as selfishness, ignorance, and democracy hold sway?

The Council was still his, and he carried the second reading by thirty-three votes to eight; but public feeling outside mastered even the Council, and in Committee he was forced to abandon the peerage proposals, accepting a nominee Upper House in their place. He managed, however, to retain provisions limiting the franchise for the other House, requiring a two-thirds majority for constitutional amendments, and—with special reference to his old enemy, Dr. Lang—excluding clergymen from membership of the legislature. Unluckily for his intentions, the Bill had to be submitted to the British Parliament, in which Robert Lowe had taken his seat in 1852, and there the two-thirds majority was reduced to a bare majority; consequently Wentworth's restrictions disappeared almost before they had become effective.

The rhetorical questions quoted above were not altogether rhetorical. In March of 1854 Wentworth left New South Wales for London, where he was deputed by the Council to help through Parliament the passage of the Enabling Bill. When it was passed with the amendment just mentioned, he knew well enough what the result would be, and did not care to face a return to a colony that would now be managed by the "arch-anarchist" Henry Parkes and his friends. The last eighteen years of his life—save for a brief eighteen months' visit to his old haunts—were spent in England,

William Charles Wentworth

where he became a member of the Conservative Club and was at one time approached to stand in the Conservative interest for Liverpool. As it happened, he could not better have reintegrated his influence in Australia. Had he returned in 1856 to the turmoil of party politics, and to a Sydney that had actually installed Parkes as its representative in his place, men would never have forgotten his struggles against popular rule. Disappearing as he did in charge of his Constitution, remembered for the next seven years only as its father and as the champion of the colony against the Colonial Office, he was able to go back in 1861 to a community that welcomed its emeritus statesman whole-heartedly. It so happened that during his visit a political crisis came about in connection with the nominee Upper House—or Legislative Council—which (as part of the compromise he had accepted) had only a five-year term of existence. To prevent bitter internecine strife Wentworth accepted from his former antagonist, Charles Cowper, the presidency of the new Council, and the turmoil ceased. Finding, however, that the Assembly (the Lower House) desired an elective Council with a low franchise, he took the first dignified opportunity of resigning his post, and in October 1862 returned to England, where for ten peaceful years he enjoyed the life of a country gentleman, and died at Wimborne, in Dorset, on 20 March, 1872. In accordance with his own wish his body was in 1873 brought to Australia; a vault was excavated in a rock near his former abode, on which he had been wont to lie gazing at the beauties of the harbour, and there, on 6 March, the coffin, brought from Sydney by the first State funeral procession in Australia, was laid in a sarcophagus, over which a small chapel has since been erected.

But the man himself lives for ever, if not in the hearts of

his countrymen—though that would be scarcely an exaggeration—at least in their institutions and their basic political ideas. He "stamped the impress of his powerful personality," says a recent biographer, "for good or evil on every political and social institution in the colony." Dr. Lang, who was at odds with him on nearly every matter that came up during their common political life, called him "one of those bodies in our solar system that are seen to throw into eclipse any body of smaller dimensions coming within the range of their vast shadow." Henry Parkes, whom he dubbed "arch-anarchist," twenty years after his death bore witness to "his indomitable efforts year after year to uplift the colony from its politically lifeless condition . . . his steady, unwearied, and enlightened labours in championing the main principles of constitutional government." The one really great change in its political mechanism that has transformed Australia since Wentworth's death—the creation of the Commonwealth—he foresaw and advocated in his Bill of 1853, which proposed "the establishment at once of a General Assembly to make laws in relation to the intercolonial questions which have arisen and may hereafter arise among" the Australian colonies; and in 1857 he submitted to the Colonial Office a proposal to let any two or more colonies federate and set up a "perambulatory" Assembly. Modern Australia, by whatever route you track back its ideas and its instrumentalities, derives from Wentworth more than from any dozen other men. He was by no means the ideal statesman; all his wisdom and foresight was apt at any moment to yield place to personal emotions, his righteous indignation to become unscrupulous and vindictive, his sense of proportion to be distorted by private friendships or enmities. But he had wisdom beyond his contemporaries, and a patriotism that has not yet been surpassed among his successors. Nor was it mere rhetoric, but sober truth, that he uttered in the outburst which is still his best epitaph:

The love of my country has been the master-passion of my life. From boyhood to manhood I have been devoted to its service; I have watched over it as a mother over her cradled child; its welfare has through life been the object of my devoted love and affection, and is still the object of my highest hopes and aspirations.

HENRY PARKES

MACQUARIE made of the Australian gaol a colony. Wentworth made it a home for free men. It was Henry Parkes who made it a democracy. Son of a farm-hand, turner by trade and Chartist by inclination, by Wentworth dubbed "arch-anarchist," he trained himself to be the friend of Robert Lowe, Alfred Tennyson, and Thomas Carlyle; he absorbed greedily not only the culture and philosophy of his friends, but the blind impulses and aspirations of the people he dwelt among, and the schemes and policies of the younger and more brilliant men with whom politics brought him into contact. He became the typical town Australian of his day, as Wentworth had become the typical up-country squatter; and, as Wentworth had done, he translated the opinions and demands of his type into something greater, more fundamental, more adjustable to world-wide conditions. Most of his work was done within the limits of a single colony, but his influence was pan-Australian, and he gave his country both a pattern scheme of primary education that still holds good and the irresistible impulse towards federation that created the Commonwealth.

Henry Parkes was born on 27 May, 1815, at Stoneleigh in Warwickshire, not far from Kenilworth. His father, a small tenant-farmer under Lord Leigh, could not provide education for his children; at the age of eight Henry was put to work near Gloucester, and his boyhood passed in squalid misery. "When Mr. Gladstone," he told a friend in later years, "was at Eton [1] preparing himself for Oxford . . . I was working at a rope-walk at fourpence a day, and suffered

[1] i.e. during the 1820's.

such cruel treatment that I was knocked down with a crowbar, and did not recover my senses for half an hour. From the rope-walk I went to labour in a brickyard, where I was again brutally used; and when Mr. Gladstone was at Oxford I was breaking stones on the Queen's highway, with hardly enough clothing to protect me from the cold." The brickyard was in Birmingham, where, after the toils just described, he found means to apprentice himself to an ivory-turner, and so made life less cruelly discomfortable. The town was then all astir with insurgent intellectualism among its artisans, who against heavy odds established mechanics' institutes to feed their brains and political unions to give them play. Henry took full advantage of both; he was an active member of the political body, which shouted for the Reform Bill of 1831 and afterwards, finding itself tricked by the Whigs, became strenuously Chartist; at the institute he battened on Shelley and Campbell — an incongruous mixture — learnt to write good English prose and mediocre but well-expressed verse, and disciplined his mind to understand and his spirit to endure whatever hardships might afflict his upward progress. Upward he was going, at whatever cost.

In Birmingham, however, the upward way seemed blocked. Lacking worldly wisdom but guided by a wiser affection, he married at twenty-one a girl whom her well-to-do parents promptly disowned. For two more years he struggled on, losing two children and experiencing dire poverty, but always bent on acquiring knowledge at all costs. That was the struggle he remembered most bitterly; pondering his past life during a long voyage to Australia, he recorded in words natural to his epoch, inflated but sincere, how

>   I have watched the children of the poor,
> Like Hunger's victims at the rich man's door,

> Who turn not from denial, jeer, or threat,
> But knock the louder, till some bread they get—
> Yes!—watched them oft, to wisdom's waters come,
> From toils ungenial, trials wearisome,
> Press through all obstacles, to gain the brink,
> Thirsting for knowledge, and resolved to drink.

At last he made up his mind to take a chance in London, and at the end of 1838 moved there with his young wife to find conditions less hopeful than ever. "It seemed as if there was no place for me," he wrote to his sister, "among the countless multitude of its inhabitants." Within a fortnight of his arrival he had determined on a greater adventure still—migration to Australia. For him, however, it was not so much an adventure as a counsel of despair:

> What drives the poor mechanic from that shore
> His sires had sooner died than left of yore?
> What drives the weeping emigrant away,
> Who leaves his home with curses on the day?
> . . . .
> Relentless misrule tears from England's breast
> Her sons who've loved and served their country best!

Four months of London—two workless, two in a woodturner's employ which brought him in about five shillings a day—whetted his longing to be away in a new country that might offer some comforts. Not that he nourished high hopes—"However I may fare on the opposite side of the globe, I do not think it can much more darken my prospects of the future." On 27 March, 1839, he and his wife left Gravesend in the *Strathfieldsaye*, travelling steerage as "bounty emigrants"—i.e. not directly assisted by the colonial Government, but brought out by masters or agents of emigrant vessels, who received from the Government a bounty on every such emigrant who should qualify under the statutory regulations. This made little difference to the travellers' comfort as passengers; probably all emigrant parties included the types that left Henry Parkes "solitary and companionless"—"this stagnant crowd of human beings, some of them of the most indecent and brutish description." But at the Sydney end of the voyage the difference was very great. Government-assisted immigrants were housed for fourteen nights after landing in properly appointed barracks; bounty immigrants were merely dumped ashore from the vessel and left to shift for themselves. The issue of the *Sydney Morning Herald* which, on 27 July, announced the *Strathfieldsaye*'s arrival in Port Jackson added an appeal to employers to engage the new-comers quickly, so as to give them a shelter at the earliest possible moment. There were 203 of them, mostly farm-labourers and dairymaids; a few house-servants, gardeners and carpenters; a printer, a lawyer, a shoemaker, a turner, a painter, a whitesmith, a saddler and a mason. Parkes, of course, was the turner. And one immigrant there was who had not been entered on the departure list; for off Cape Howe on 23 July a child was born to him.

It was perhaps as well that Henry had not sailed high-heartedly to his new country, for his first experiences of it were almost disastrous. He reached Sydney with three shillings in his pocket, and had to leave his wife and child aboard while he hunted for shelter; after a few days she

was obliged to go on shore, with her newborn infant in her arms, and to walk a mile across the town of Sydney to the miserable place I had been able to provide for her as a home, which was a little, low, dirty, unfurnished room without a fireplace, at five shillings per week rent.

A fortnight of this, made possible only by the sale of a few tools and possessions he had brought from England drove, him to take work as a farm-labourer thirty-six miles inland, where for toil from sunrise to sunset he was to receive £25 a year with a ration and a half of food. The weekly ration is worth noting:

    10¼ lb. of beef, sometimes unfit to eat.
    10½ lb. rice, of the worst imaginable quality.
    6¾ lb. flour, half made up of ground rice.
    2 lb. sugar, good-tasted brown.
    ¼ lb. tea, inferior.
    ¼ lb. soap, not enough to wash our hands.
    2 figs of tobacco, useless to me.

(The comments are, of course, Henry's. He adds: "Not a leaf of a vegetable or a drop of milk beyond this.") Six months of these conditions, ending with the toilsome vintage season, carried him through the summer; then he made back to Sydney, obtained work in an ironmonger's store, passed from that to a brass-foundry, and from that to employment in the Customs as a tide-waiter. There first he began to enjoy life a little. From the ironmongery he had written home that

I have been disappointed in all my expectations of Australia, except as to its wickedness; for it is far more wicked than I had conceived it possible for any place to be, or than it is possible for me to describe to you in England.

By September 1840, momentarily safe in the Customs ("I spend most of my time on board ships, where I have a good deal of leisure to write poetry"), he was saving money, and by the following May had begun to make the acquaintance of well-to-do merchants and politicians, but was not yet reconciled to Australian life; he thought of re-visiting England, possibly by way of Java. In August of 1841 he was "quite happy"; in September of 1842, after a year of insolvencies and slack work that affected even the Customs, he was again contemplating a fresh migration—to New Zealand, or Tahiti, or Chile, or Malacca, or the United States, anywhere for a change; the only use he had for England was "to lay my bones there at last." His restlessness affected his work; in 1843 he began to complain to his superiors about malpractices and improper proceedings in the department, and made himself unpopular thereby. Whether or no his complaints were justified is not clear, but his next step was resignation, and in 1844 he invested his savings in a small shop in Kent Street, where he made and sold toys and other goods turned by himself from ivory or bone. This speculation proved successful enough to ensure him a living, and leisure to make friends and interest himself in public affairs. He talked no more of leaving Australia, and began to contribute both verse and prose to Robert Lowe's *Atlas*, where he joined a remarkable band of writers: James Martin, afterwards Premier of the colony and Chief Justice; Thomas Mitchell, the Surveyor-General; Archibald Michie (power behind the throne in many Victorian ministries); William Forster (most cultured of New South Wales politicians); William Sharp Macleay, the man of science—few editors, even in London, have driven so good a team. Parkes's contributions were chiefly made to the Poets' Corner, for he was still emulous of the bays, had become intimate with the local poet, Charles Harpur, and had already in 1842 published a slim volume of very so-so verse (*Stolen Moments*), dedicated to his head in the Customs, James Gibbes, and prefaced with a list of 113 subscribers ranging from the Lieutenant-Governor down to Andrew Polack of the cheap store, Sydney's early Victorian Woolworth.

We have considered his early life thus fully because it

became and remained the indelible background to his adult political ideas. Never in his life could he forget the dreary, desperate months that followed his arrival in Sydney, or regard without distrust and dislike the up-country landowners who thought more of their stock than of their labourers. And the remedies he advocated, the panaceas he sought, were drawn from his Birmingham days, when

> I hung upon the voice of Daniel O'Connell with an unspeakable interest. . . . I felt myself moulded like wax in the heat of the splendid declamation of George Thompson, the anti-slavery orator. . . . I was amongst the listeners to the wild lectures of Charles Pemberton. These were my teachers, together with the living poets of the time, such as Byron, Moore, Shelley, and Leigh Hunt.

After four years of watching and studying, he suddenly broke into the political arena with a daring gesture. At the elections of 1848 a proposed revival of transportation (which had ceased, so far as concerned New South Wales, in 1841) was the chief issue; William Wentworth, its defender, and his friend, William Bland, were the official candidates for Sydney. Robert Lowe, the ablest opponent of the proposals, on 1 July announced his candidature for a constituency in the far south of the colony, which he had already represented. Parkes, without Lowe's leave and apparently on his own initiative, nominated Lowe for one of the Sydney seats, acted as secretary for the excited canvass that followed, and succeeded without the slightest assistance from the candidate in procuring him a good majority over Bland and a bare minority below Wentworth. The shock to the pro-transportation squatters' clique then in power was very great, and they were still more alarmed when in June 1849 the arrival of a vessel containing convicts (the notorious *Hashemy*) in Port Jackson aroused a portentous demonstration of seven thousand citizens at Circular Quay to protest against the landing of the detested transportees. Lowe was again the leader; after him a young ivory-turner spoke avowedly as the mouthpiece "of the largest class in the colony — the working-class," and made himself from that moment the spokesman of Australian democracy. Lowe was no democrat—only Wentworth's spasmodic divergences into pure squattocracy drove him temporarily into that camp. But Parkes on Hashemy Day came into his own, and never again entirely lost the allegiance of the artisan-labourer section of the community.

The campaign against transportation was not his only or his chief interest. That was merely one side of his attack on the privileged position of the colony's landowners, and he proceeded to strengthen it by founding a newspaper. The *Empire*, which first appeared (as a weekly) on 28 December, 1850, stood for a wide extension of the franchise, a redistribution of electorates based on population—thus increasing the townsfolk's influence over that of the squatters—cheap and widespread popular education, and greatly retrenched taxation. Within a month it was converted to a daily paper, and was well on its way to prosperity when the discovery of gold sent wages soaring, and gravely affected every city enterprise that had not large reserves of capital at its back. Parkes's compositors struck work and were sent to prison for it, but without imperilling his popularity; he imported fresh compositors, some from England, others from the Eurasian community of Madras, but lost not a follower thereby; only, from that time onward he struggled in vain against imminent insolvency, and in 1858 was compelled to sell the venture and accept "absolute ruin to my worldly prospects." "The seven years of continuous labour," he wrote in 1891, "have remained a blank in my existence"

—all he recollected was "days and nights together without sleep at all."

It is not necessary to attribute all this misfortune to the gold-rush. A moderately capable journalist—under direction—Parkes was the last man in the world to make a good editor or manager. He was of the type that modern slang calls "temperamental," and lacked all his life the steady, sober judgment, the poise, the sense of proportion, that is requisite for good press management. Moreover, he was not single-minded in the business; in May 1854 he succeeded Wentworth (much to the latter's disgust) as a representative of Sydney in the old Council, in 1856 was second among its four elected representatives in the new Council, resigned at the end of the year, was re-elected early in 1858, resigned again (how temperamental!) before the end of that year, was elected for East Sydney in 1859, and resigned for the third time in 1861—this time for good reason. He took both his occupations seriously:

I would leave the Council when it adjourned and go to the *Empire* office, where I would remain until daylight. Day and night I was at work. Very often I was thirty-six and forty-eight hours without going to bed.

One need scarcely seek any other cause for the newspaper's failure. But it did good work of a kind while it lasted; it helped to kill Wentworth's fantastic House of Lords, it was a rallying-point for working-class opinion and a source of adequate leadership, and it spurred on its sober and "stodgy" rivals of less democratic views to enliven their columns and clear their brains.[1] Parkes himself during those years did valuable work also in the legislature. He began his

[1] The *Empire* did not die when Parkes sold it, though its character was considerably altered. In its new phase it lived respectably until 1875.

career there by advocating a more liberal system of immigration, the establishment of a nautical school in Port Jackson, and the investigation of (*a*) attempts to import coolie labour for squatters, and (*b*) the apparently hopeless failure of agriculture in the colony; each of these beginnings was to bear fruit in later years. The new legislature of 1856 was chiefly occupied with revising details of the new Constitution and providing for the separation of Queensland, but Parkes found opportunity to revive his advocacy of immigration and to urge insistently that a national militia should be substituted for the British garrison which still defended the colony. For a time he worked shoulder to shoulder with John Robertson, a squatter, who had cut himself aloof from his kind when Wentworth began to demand freehold tenure of outback runs, and who had developed a taste for radical policies of the Parkes type—manhood suffrage, voting by ballot, State-endowed education, and, above all, "free selection" of land (i.e. the right of any man to pick out of the huge area leased to squatters a small block of land, purchasable by instalments under condition of three years' residence and the making of a few improvements). This system of land-settlement, which did a little good and a great deal of harm,[1] was in the end copied in

---

[1] I may perhaps be permitted to quote my own criticism of it from a textbook used widely in Australia:

"Few laws, one hopes, have done as much harm to the community as this Land Act of 1861. Its ostensible object—the settling of small farmers on the fertile patches of land—was rarely attained; in twenty-two years over 60,000 applications were made under it, and of them more than two-thirds were either dummies or failures, the land falling back into the big runs. It divided the country population into two hostile camps, each hating and suspecting the other. And its moral effect is best described in the words of a Royal Commission's report: 'It has

most of the other colonies; in New South Wales it was carried after severe fighting and a constitutional crisis, largely because of the backing given to it by Parkes and the section of public opinion which took its guidance from him.

Immigration was still his chief interest, however, and in May 1861 he persuaded Parliament to appoint "missioners" to England for its encouragement. Robertson, who was already a little inconvenienced by his backer's temperament, and the then Premier—Charles Cowper, a politician of considerable acumen, usually known as "Slippery Charley" —saw their chance, and offered him an appointment as one of the delegation. At the end of May he left Parliament, and in August reached Liverpool with his colleague, William Bede Dalley. The fourteen-months' mission that ensued —Dalley taking the Home Counties and Ireland, Parkes Scotland and Western and Northern England—was of no great importance to the colony that dispatched it, since the delegates could only advocate migration without offering any assistance to the intending migrants. To Parkes himself it was of inestimable value. He met on equal terms—he, who never forgot he had been a farmer's boy and had almost starved in London—not only politicians of the calibre of John Pakington and Richard Cobden and John Bright (who, by the way, disliked emigration), but also Thomas Carlyle, who had, as readers of *Latter-Day Pamphlets* (if there are any nowadays) will remember, ideas peculiarly his own about colonisation. The friendship then begun lasted a lifetime, and gave Parkes the assured self-respect

tarnished the personal virtues of veracity and honourable dealing by the daily habit of intrigue, by the practice of evading the law, and by declarations in defiance of fact universally made.'"— *History of Australia*, pp. 234-5.

that he had till then lacked; some of its manifestations were quaint, as when Carlyle, asked for a list of authors worth special attention, suggested—in writing, so that the choice was deliberate—Pope, Swift, Shenstone, Goldsmith, Smollett, Benjamin Franklin, Camden's *Britannia*, and the *Heimskringla*.

In October 1862 Parkes returned to Sydney, and for a while lived unobtrusively, watching the political rise and fall of a Cowper-Robertson combination alternately with a Martin-Forster combination, the latter a relic of the old *Atlas* group. After two unsuccessful attempts to re-enter Parliament, he was returned in April 1864 by the small coastal constituency of Kiama, and provisionally supported Cowper, but refused to take office under him next year because of his unprogressive attitude towards popular education. This interest now so filled Parkes's mind that when Cowper's Ministry fell he joined Martin—with whose fiscal beliefs he heartily disagreed—in a Ministry that set itself, against extreme denominational opposition, to remodel the whole State system of education. Martin established industrial schools and a "juvenile reformatory"; Parkes created "public" schools of a non-sectarian character, under trained teachers, whose standards were henceforth to hold good in all denominational schools that might desire State support. To administer the system he established a Council of Education, with himself as President, which included the Premier, the Speaker, and a professor of the university as members. Further, he made sure that the intention and working of the scheme should be thoroughly understood, by seizing every chance (and a colonial Minister has many) of explaining to audiences at banquets, election meetings, openings of new school-buildings, and so on, exactly what the Act meant and what must be done under it.

His toil was rewarded: no Act ever passed in New South Wales was better understood or more popular, and its popularity ensured his. Determined that no child in the colony of his adoption should suffer the enforced ignorances of his own youth, he thus seized his first opportunity of real power to found a type-system of education for all Australia; vastly improved and extended, it is still the basis of the systems of to-day.

His thirty-two months' tenure of office under Martin included two exciting episodes whose memory stuck to him. He had to face in 1866 a peculiarly vicious outbreak of bushranging, during which five policemen were killed (a rare phenomenon in the bushranging of those years), and which was suppressed only by the Minister's personal interference and choice of a police leader. And in 1868, during a visit of the then Duke of Edinburgh to Sydney, an Irish lad newly arrived in the colony shot him, creating a violent panic among local politicians. Parkes, who was official head of the police, remained calmer than most; but while the outrage was still fresh he took occasion to address his constituents at Kiama, and to assure them that O'Farrell's crime was the outcome of a plot connected with Fenianism, and not remotely alien from the Roman Catholic Irish in Australia.[1] This rash and unwarranted imputation on a strong and resentful section of the colonists, already antagonised by the effect of his education scheme on Roman Catholic schools, hampered the whole of Parkes's later career; for anyone who desired to rouse Irish opposition to any measure he chose to bring forward need henceforth only mention "The Kiama Ghost," and the trick was done.

[1] Those interested may read the full details in Parkes's *Fifty Years of Australian History* (vol. i., pp. 221–39), a book on which I have drawn liberally in this sketch.

From September 1868 to the beginning of 1871 he sat in opposition, still representing Kiama. Then, in a fit of temper, he suddenly resigned his seat [1] and betook himself to journalism. The circumstances are unimportant in themselves, but his account of them is too characteristically naïve to be overlooked:

My first speech was delivered in condemnation of the appointment of Agent-General. The leading journal of the colony next morning came out with a volley of abuse against me for my speech; admitting that the appointment was bad, said the critic, I was not the person to condemn it. Incredible as it may appear to strangers, and Quixotic as it appears to myself at this distance of time, I thereupon resigned the seat to which I had just been so handsomely elected. Without taking time for calm reflection, I contended that, if I could not deal with all questions with unimpaired privilege and untrammelled judgment, I ought not to be in the House at all.

For more than a year he kept clear of active politics, making a living partly by journalism, partly as representative of a new line of steamers intended to trade between Sydney and San Francisco. But in January 1872 he secured a seat in Parliament from the western country electorate of Mudgee, leaving it almost at once (for he was never really comfortable as a country representative) to regain the East Sydney seat which he had held in the 'fifties. At once he stepped into the front rank of New South Wales politicians, and on 9 May was commissioned to form a Ministry, which lasted, despite the bitter attacks of James Martin and John Robertson (two of his former colleagues), the better part of three years. Martin was soon removed from

[1] He actually resigned twice in that year—first in October, because he had been declared insolvent; a second time, after his re-election early in November, on the excuse stated above.

Parliament to become Chief Justice—an appointment all the more gratifying to its maker because he both lost an antagonist and gave the country a great judge. Robertson became leader of the Opposition, and there ensued the same see-saw between him and Parkes as had occurred in the 'sixties between Cowper and Martin. During his first premiership Parkes achieved little except the abolition of certain customs duties which seemed to him to taint his Free Trade policy, and was thrown out of office on a peculiarly irrelevant issue—the release, after ten years' imprisonment, of a notable bushranger, which had been recommended by the Chief Justice and personally approved by the Governor.

Probably the most interesting episode (to him) of these years was his forlorn attempt to draw W. E. Gladstone into taking some interest in the colonies. Already contemplating a not very distant federation of Australia, he suggested that Gladstone (who had just been driven from power) should think about conferring on the Australian colonies "a higher political status." No one knows what he meant, and certainly Gladstone did not; his reply was that no one in England wanted to interfere with colonial self-government—which was, no doubt, true, but seems remote from any meaning Parkes could possibly have; and Parkes in despair retorted that "England, as represented by her eminent men, and by her literature, forms no adequate conception of our importance," adding a suggestion that Gladstone should study a gazetteer. Such may be the futility of two eminent politicians when arguing at a range of twelve thousand miles.

Two years in opposition, during which Robertson did less than Parkes had done, a five months' return to office and another four months of opposition, during which nobody did anything except quarrel at the country's expense, sickened the electors of the see-saw. At the elections of December 1877 neither leader procured a majority, and for twelve months both were out of office, and had time to think about sinking their differences. So at the end of 1878 they coalesced, defeated the amiable gentleman who had been stopping the gap, and began a four-years' joint rule which endowed New South Wales with a second Education Act and Australia with the beginnings of federation. The revision of the Education Act of 1866, which Parkes always considered one of his best achievements, was brought about by an unexpected attack on the system made in June 1879 by the Roman Catholic hierarchy, who denounced the State's schools as "seedplots of future immorality, infidelity and lawlessness." Parkes replied by abolishing all State aid to denominational schools and instituting a purely unsectarian system under control of a Minister; religious teaching might be given for an hour a week in the public-school building by anyone his Church chose to authorise; attendance at some school, or in the child's home under some tutor or governess, was made compulsory in all settled districts. The Act with minor amendments still holds good in New South Wales—so, too, does the grievance of the Roman Catholic community, whose leaders have never ceased to demand the restoration of subsidies to all Catholic schools that prove themselves by any adequate test as efficient on the secular side as the State's schools. Other denominations have acquiesced in the Act, but not they.

Two other proposals of lasting importance stand to Parkes's credit during this term of office. In 1880–1 he advocated at conferences between the colonial Premiers legislation restricting drastically the influx of Chinese into Australia, and put such an Act into the New South Wales statute-book. And at the conference of 1881 he brought forward a provisional scheme (which he afterwards abandoned) for prefacing any real Federal movement by the creation of a "Federal Council" with very limited powers. Both these tentative gestures were to lead to serious action later; for the time Parkes was prevented by illness from proceeding farther with them, and at the end of 1881 left Sydney on a prolonged journey through the United States and Europe. Returning to Australia in August 1882, he found that the coalition was doomed, Robertson having alienated many supporters by an attempt to patch up his old and discredited land policy instead of reforming it altogether. The Ministry was heavily defeated; Alexander Stuart, who had put forward a land-reform scheme of his own, took office to carry it through; and Parkes went back to America and Europe.

These two visits to the older world heartened him mightily, and widened his political outlook to the great advantage of the Empire. Always haunted by the shadows of his miserable childhood, he learnt that England was not the anti-democratic bogey he had too often conjured up; he found himself (and was legitimately proud to find himself) an honoured guest of Governors and Chief Justices and a President in the United States, of Gladstone and Tennyson, Browning and Owen, the Royal Academy and the Royal Family in England. Of the non-political friendships he was especially proud, for he knew they must be personal, and hoped they were due to his literary production—vain hope, for his written work rarely reached mediocrity and never soared above it [1]; it

[1] It is a perpetual astonishment to students of his career that the statesman who could remodel a colony after his own desire, drag together six quarrelling and jealous legislatures to contemplate federal union, and win—and deserve—the friendship of

was his intellectual vigour and remarkable career that made him worth the friendship of soberer and more assiduously trained intellects.

By August 1884 he was back in Sydney, watching the political situation with languid interest, and two months later decided to resign the seat for the northern country constituency of Tenterfield, which he had held during his absences in Europe. As usual, he had scarcely settled down to private work when startling news summoned him back to the political arena. Gordon was dead in Khartoum; Australia, not understanding — but whole-heartedly disapproving—the policy which had left him there unsupported, was moved to display in some fashion her feelings about his loss. On 12 February, 1885, Dalley (then Attorney-General and acting-Premier) persuaded the New South Wales Cabinet to offer a contingent of artillery and infantry for service in the Sudan. On the 15th the offer was accepted by the British Government, and on 3 March the troops sailed. Victoria, South Australia and Queensland also offered troops, but these were declined with thanks on the ground that the delay needed to organise so many contingents would jeopardise the success of the expedition they were intended to join in. Dalley's action was, on the whole, popular, but Parkes felt moved to condemn it—his reasons were not clear, but one cannot help thinking that he was actuated partly by his admiration for Gladstone, and felt that the offer implied (as it did) a disapproval of Gladstone's

Carlyle and Tennyson, should be content to offer the world as part of his contribution to poetry:

> "I would not give my ragged Jane
>   For all the peacock ladies going.
> She knows the way to banish pain—
>   What she don't know is not worth knowing."

previous lack of action. To test the feeling of the country he took the earliest opportunity of contesting an election, and on 17 March was returned by a small majority for the country constituency of Argyle, claiming the result (probably due to his personal reputation) as a proof that his attack on Dalley represented public feeling. Back in harness, he soon abandoned his country electorate—as in 1872—and drove the newest Premier, George Dibbs, from his seat at North Sydney. The Dibbs Ministry fell promptly, to be succeeded by a two-months' Robertson Ministry and one that survived for eleven months under Sir Patrick Jennings. Parkes sat by scornfully while Jennings strove to control a Cabinet of discordances; when it collapsed in January 1887, he was called back to office by the Governor and found himself facing a hostile House. He asked for a month's supply, and was accorded a vote of censure; hurriedly obtaining from the Governor an immediate dissolution, he faced the House again, dared it to refuse him three months' supply, got the vote, dissolved the Parliament, and went raging through the country to rally his supporters—acquiring in the new Parliament a majority of fourteen.

These details, unimportant in themselves, may help to reconstruct the picture of Parkes at his strongest. He was seventy-one, and worn with nearly forty years of bitter political fighting; he had powerful enemies, and friends who depended on him for their strength instead of strengthening him. Yet he won through by sheer force of will. I shall not easily forget his appearance at Bathurst, then represented by a man whom he had lifted into office and who had afterwards turned Protectionist and joined Dibbs. Fresh from his conflict with the now cowed House, he told the dramatic story in a high, piping voice—utterly alien from the leonine head and dominating stand of him—that struck one as absurd till it gripped and controlled his audience; and every time he hissed out the name "Suttor" it sounded, and felt, more like "Satan." This was the beginning of a startling two-years' term of power, during which he remodelled the tariff, created bodies outside ministerial control to manage the State railways and initiate the construction of public works, obtained Parliament's assent to the agreement that gave Australia a small squadron of her own, and established firmly on its true and sound basis the doctrine of White Australia. Locally his biggest achievement at this time was his creation of a Board of Railway Commissioners independent of political influence or control. This was a new departure in a country where State ownership of public utilities and State interference in many businesses was familiar, and usually connoted political control and the bestowal of patronage by politicians. It took both courage and hard fighting to loosen the grip of Parliament on the State's most important business mechanism; indeed, the mere creation of the Board would have availed little had not Parkes made himself its spokesman in Parliament and established the precedent of defending its independence against all attacks, even those of his own colleagues. The inestimable value of this precedent will be understood best by those who care to study the development in after years of a similar body, the Public Service Board, which was not thus protected by its creators against the attempts of politicians to influence its decisions.[1] The body concerned with public works was of a

[1] Parkes's political acumen was shown in this connection by his refusal to burden the Board with the power of deciding on new construction. The extension of railways into districts unable for a time to make them pay is a recognised and legitimate branch of railway business in Australia, since development is more needed there than monetary profits. Business managers chosen for their knowledge of railways can hardly be expected to select

different kind, merely a standing committee of both Houses of Parliament empowered to examine rigorously every proposal for constructing any work that is to cost more than £20,000, and to suspend for a year at least any construction which it disapproves. The Naval Agreement had already been formulated at the Colonial Conference of 1887, and Parkes's share in it was simply to persuade his legislature to accept it, which he did with little trouble and a praiseworthy comprehension of its implications.

His most significant work during this term of office, from the Imperial standpoint, was his handling of the problem of Chinese immigration. As has been said above, he had in 1881 strictly limited the number of these immigrants—not because he believed them inferior to Australians, but because he thought them "incapable of assimilation in the body politic, strangers to our civilisation, out of sympathy with our aspirations, and unfitted for our free institutions." Incompatibility, not inferiority — this was the point he always stressed:

They are a superior set of people . . . a nation of an old and deep-rooted civilisation. . . . It is for these qualities I do not want them to come here. The influx of a few millions of Chinese would entirely change the character of this young Australian commonwealth. It is because I believe the Chinese to be a powerful race, capable of taking a great hold upon the country, and because I wish to preserve the type of my own nation in these fair countries, that I am and always have been opposed to the influx of Chinese.

In 1886 the Chinese Government had begun to take an

such districts of their own knowledge, and political influence is bound to creep in. A Board of Railway Commissioners set up in Victoria was given (nominally) the power of selection—with the result that its chief was discredited and dismissed for wasting public money on new railway lines which had really been forced on him by politicians.

active interest in the attempts to exclude its nationals from British colonies, in 1887 had sent a commission to Australia to investigate the trouble there, and towards the end of the year had protested in London against the exclusion laws. To test British and colonial feeling an exceptionally large number of Chinese were allowed to leave for Australia early in 1888, some eager to exploit newly discovered ruby mines in the Northern Territory, others swarming towards the settled areas of the south-east. Before the end of May four vessels reached Port Jackson, bringing about six hundred Chinese, and a demonstration headed by the Mayor of Sydney clamoured outside Parliament House against letting them land. Parkes had already made up his mind. On 31 March he had cabled to the Foreign Office a request that exclusion should be arranged by treaty with the Chinese Government. In face of the latest incursion he decided to take instant action, and introduced a Bill restricting immigration more drastically than ever (raising, for instance, the entrance tax from £10 to £100 per head); and, irritated by the fact that the Foreign Office had not troubled even to acknowledge his March message, he defied the British Government to force aliens on the colony against its will:

> Neither for Her Majesty's ships of war, nor for Her Majesty's representative on the spot, nor for the Secretary of State for the Colonies, do we intend to turn aside from our purpose, which is to terminate the landing of Chinese on these shores for ever, except under the restrictions imposed by this Bill, which will amount, and which are intended to amount, to practical prohibition.

With an amendment easing the situation of Chinese already resident in New South Wales, the Bill became law. In June the Australian Premiers met in conference, but achieved little, though the Colonial Office gave them a hint (which was taken in later years) that the least obnoxious method of procedure was to restrict, nominally, the immigration of all foreigners "with power of relaxing the regulations in certain cases." However, there was no further need of laws or of treaties when a decision of the Privy Council admitted that any self-governing colony had the power to exclude aliens from its ports if the public peace would be endangered by their admission.

In January 1889 the fourth Parkes Ministry was defeated on a motion relating to the Railway Board, and George Dibbs went to the country as Premier on a Protectionist platform. He was defeated by a narrow majority, and Parkes came back with a Cabinet of new men, whose two and a half years of power produced little legislation of importance but provided a pattern of excellent administration. It was about this time that Sir Charles Dilke, summing up recollections of several visits to Australia within the previous twenty years, penned a striking if prejudiced description of the "patriarch among colonial politicians":

> Sir Henry Parkes, who has something of the aspect of Mr. Punch's Father Thames, but with a clean beard . . . has retired from public life more often than a popular actor from the stage, and the occasional raffles of his effects have not lessened the number of his political admirers. Sir Henry Parkes believes in himself, and that deep self-belief undoubtedly impresses many of those about him and makes them too believe. . . . In person he has been as little favoured by nature with good looks as Socrates or Darwin. For all that, there is an assurance of strength in the massy features, and a consciousness in the eyes that their owner is not an ordinary man. The fact is that, with all his faults and all his weaknesses, Sir Henry Parkes is the only great political power in New South Wales. His sympathy with the democratic ideas which are uppermost in Australia, and his devotion to the colony and broad grasp of affairs, give him a greater hold upon the people than any other Australian public man. His debts, his poetry, are powerless to sink him, and as a man who knows how

to use, like so many chessmen, the sections which take the place of parties in colonial politics, he is undoubtedly one of the ablest of colonial politicians.—*Problems of Greater Britain*, i. 289, 293.

This appreciation of the old leader, excellent as far as it goes, is marred by a bias which Dilke could hardly have escaped. His hero at the time was Dalley, and he regarded the dispatch of troops to the Sudan by Dalley as one of the finest Imperialistic gestures yet made outside Britain. He could not, therefore, rightly understand the man who had protested against the Sudan expedition and had brought a large section of electors to agree with him; his information was mainly derived from Dalley's friends, and from Imperialists in the other colonies who could not swallow Parkes's defiance of the British Government over the exclusion of Chinese. This bias shows itself almost brazenly in the astonishing statement (on p. 290) that

in a colony which as a whole is jealous of Victoria he is the person who is most jealous,

followed by a suggestion that Parkes's anti-Chinese policy was largely dictated by a resolve to outdo Victoria in violence. As we have seen already, that policy was based on Parkes's personal convictions and on them alone, just as his refusal to join the "rickety" Federal Council (discussed below) was based not on distrust of Victoria, but on a firm determination to be satisfied with nothing less than the best form of Federation. But the Victorians of those years, obsessed with the belief that New South Wales was seething with jealousy of their prosperity and their wisdom, and bitterly resenting John Robertson's notorious gibe at their "cabbage-garden" of a colony, saw in his former colleague's slightest action a direct attack on themselves; and Dilke's understanding of their bogey could not rise above its source.

Parkes by this time had greater schemes in his mind than

any rivalries between colony and colony. As far back as 1867 he had assumed the successorship to Wentworth as an advocate of Federation. He repeated his creed in the correspondence with Gladstone in 1874. During his administration of 1880–3 he brought up the subject at various inter-colonial conferences, obtaining the support of South Australia and Tasmania but failing to convince Victoria and Queensland. Then in 1883 Queensland's annexation of southern New Guinea and the prompt disavowal of her action by the British Government forced upon those recalcitrant colonies the disadvantages of disunion; in June the Victorian Premier demanded immediate federation, in July the Queensland Executive Council asked the Imperial Parliament to take the matter up, in November an inter-colonial conference, at the instigation of the two recent converts, invented a "Federal Council" to act for Australia as a whole on certain matters of external policy. Parkes was away in England just then, but on his return flatly condemned the proposed Council (which he himself, before his visit to England, had suggested) as inadequate and inefficient, and persuaded New South Wales to stand out. In this he proved himself indubitably a statesman, not merely an able or a clever politician. Among the Australians of that type, able and skilful enough in their own narrow colonial world, he was the one man who saw Australia clearly in its relation to the Empire and the world at large. They hoped that their provisional, parochial Council, with its limited powers and its complete and lasting dependence on the various colonial legislatures, would fulfil well enough the immediate purposes of its founders, concentrating to some extent the Australian effort towards mastery in the western Pacific and speaking to Britain as a people's voice. Parkes knew better. His long experience of Colonial Secretaries and his native good sense in Imperial affairs told him that so weak, so ephemeral, so unstable a body could neither formulate a permanent policy in external affairs, nor gain attention in London, should its attempts at policy conflict with the mightier and more persistent influence of ambitious European nations. Nothing less than a genuine and permanent Federal Parliament, free from the jealousies of seven small colonies (for at that time it was thought that New Zealand might join in) and speaking as the direct voice of the whole Australian population, would satisfy either Parkes or the British Government. Until he saw a chance of establishing that sort of Federation, he was content to wait, and to keep his colony waiting with him.

Neither had to wait long. In 1889, having formed his fifth Ministry and found nothing particular for it to do, he recurred to the subject of Federation in a correspondence with Duncan Gillies, then Premier of Victoria, who at once snubbed him; no one wanted Federation, he said—if Parkes wanted it, why did he not join the Federal Council? In October, however, was published a report on the defences of the Australian colonies by an Imperial officer, Major-General Bevan Edwards, which strongly recommended the consolidation of the six weak defence forces into a single Australian army. Parkes seized his chance, and six days later invited the other Premiers to a conference. Again Gillies snubbed him; this time he met the snub with a call to the people behind all premiers. From his speech at Tenterfield in northern New South Wales, made on 24 October, dates the great campaign that eventually created the Commonwealth. Luckily we have an eyewitness's description of the man at his greatest:

> The excellent choice of words, the masterly elaboration of phrases, which were obviously moulded while he stood there upon

his feet, were in some contrast to the manner of his utterance. The voice was a little veiled by fatigue and age. The massive shoulders were a little bowed; but the huge head, with its streaming wave of silver hair and beard, was held as erect as ever. The rough homely features were as eloquent as the words he spoke; and the instinct of a natural fighting man lit up the ancient warrior's eye. The mere aspect and manner would have been remarkable to a stranger anywhere; but there, where for the first time the voice of an authoritative statesman gave soul and utterance to the aspirations of a people, it was truly remarkable and not without a touch of sublimity.—David Christie Murray, *The Cockney Columbus*, p. 277.

The speech rang through Australia, and before its echoes had ceased Parkes struck hard. On 30 October, and again on 4 November, he sent an appeal to all the Premiers; when they replied after the Gillies fashion, professing to believe that everything he wanted could still be attained through the Federal Council, he appealed once more to the electors (on the 6th and the 22nd), and on the 26th inserted in the Governor's speech at the opening of a legislative session at Sydney an optimistic reference to "the birth of a nation." A third circular dispatch to the other Premiers followed immediately—and the affair was settled. In February 1890 thirteen representatives of seven colonies met in Melbourne, resolved

that the best interests and the present and future prosperity of the Australian colonies will be promoted by an early union under the Crown,

and agreed to persuade their respective legislatures to

appoint delegates to a National Australian Convention, empowered to consider and report upon an adequate scheme for a Federal Constitution.

During the conference two celebrated phrases were coined, when James Service, an ex-Premier of Victoria, spoke of the fiscal problem as "the lion in the path," and Henry Parkes, before answering that "this question of a common tariff is a mere trifle compared with the overshadowing question of living an eternal national existence," paused in his attack to remind the still disunited colonies that "the crimson thread of kinship runs through us all."

There is no need here to recapitulate the often-told story of the long Federal campaign. Its initiation has been worth recording in detail to show the enthusiasm and acumen which Parkes could summon to his aid when well into his seventies. The rest of the story, as far as it concerns him, is rather pitiful. Few politicians could rise to Parkes's contempt of the lion in the path. In his own colony his own supporters feared the abandonment of Free Trade more than they desired Australian unity; one of them drew an awesome picture of the devastation that must ensue—"South Australia will get Broken Hill and our silver-mines. Victoria will get Riverina. Queensland will take our sugar-lands, and we shall be left with a ridge of mountains and nothing else to govern." While the New South Wales Parliament was in the middle of a debate on the proposed Convention, Parkes was thrown out of a runaway cab and broke his right leg. From that moment he lost his nerve, and never again met difficulties with a high heart and a determined resolution. The debate lagged in his absence, but by September his proposals for a Convention were carried and the New South Wales delegates chosen—Parkes himself, of course, and six other members of Parliament representing all shades of opinion. On 2 March, 1891, the National Australasian Convention met at Sydney, and the old leader mastered his increasing physical weakness enough to preside over it and to take a very active part in the debates; but he lacked energy from the start, having been compelled by his six colleagues to modify considerably the resolutions on which he wished to found the new Australia. He had hoped to endow the new nation with the bulk of its still unoccupied lands, reserving to existing colonies all the territory they had hitherto been able to utilise; anyone who has studied the history of migration to Australia since 1901 can easily surmise how lamentable it has been that this suggestion was rejected. Instead, the colonies were confirmed in the full possession of their territorial rights, and the Commonwealth to-day is unable to develop a systematic immigration policy because the land for which settlers are needed is under the control of six States with six not very harmonious schemes of their own. However, the main part of his work was accepted, Federation was agreed to, and a Federal Constitution was drawn up.

Then a fatal mistake was made. The Convention, instead of referring its Constitution to the several parliaments for discussion, asked them merely to make provision for submitting it to the people for approval. The point may seem trivial nowadays; at the moment, while Federation was not popularly understood and everything depended on the caprice of six legislatures, a proposal to use them as transmitting instruments rather than as coadjutor-advisers militated strongly against the success of the campaign. The other colonies waited on New South Wales, since her stedfast adherence to Free Trade was the crux of the whole problem. Six weeks after the Convention had risen Parkes submitted the draft Constitution Bill to his Parliament, making it clear—for he had seen the danger—that discussion of details would be allowed. He soon discovered that members were in no temper to handle the Bill thoughtfully, and he could no longer raise in himself the fiery zeal which had mastered other equally recalcitrant Houses; he faltered, postponed the Bill in favour of more immediately interesting local subjects (local government and electoral reform), and was unexpectedly forced to a dissolution. The new Parliament was a severe blow to him, and to Federation. Three parties suddenly appeared in it, his own numbering forty-eight, a direct Opposition numbering fifty-six, and a Labour section of thirty; only with Labour's help could he carry on at all, and, when that was withdrawn because of his attitude on an eight-hours question, he threw up the sponge and left office for the last time. The cause of Federation he bequeathed to an able but indolent assistant, Edmund Barton, who took office in the new Protectionist Ministry but dallied a year before re-introducing the Bill for further discussion. By that time public feeling had occupied itself with other matters, the other colonies had grown tired of waiting for dilatory New South Wales, and Federation was shelved indefinitely.

Parkes for his part sank thankfully back into private life and began to write up his memoirs. What attention he still paid to politics was devoted to hatred of George Reid, a comparatively young champion of Free Trade who, though nominally a Federationist, had hampered him continuously by flaunting the fiscal objection to all practical schemes for union, and had succeeded him (to his great disgust) as leader of the anti-Protectionists in the legislature. [Possibly Parkes then began to understand how Wentworth had felt when the "arch-anarchist" succeeded him as member for Sydney in 1854.] He made a few appearances in the House, assertively independent (he had publicly refused to follow the new leader), made one futile attempt on a motion for adjournment to revive the Federation problem,[1] and then

[1] His proposal on this occasion, though it met with no favour then, was identical with that adopted by Reid in 1895—that a

lay back disheartened, licking his wounds. A worse wound was inflicted on him when in 1894 the Protectionist Ministry was defeated and the Governor sent for Reid, although a majority of the party had decided to recall Parkes to the leadership. The old man felt the blow very deeply. He endeavoured to regain his position as leader of the Federationists by moving to resume the debate on the half-forgotten Bill; Reid countered the move by accepting Federation, offering himself as leader, and calling a Premiers' Conference to adopt the principle of a popularly elected Convention. While preparations were being made for this, he interested his legislature in two proposals of extreme local importance—land taxation and reform of the nominee Upper House; Parkes vainly tried by allying himself temporarily with the Protectionists to oust Reid and regain his hold on the Federal movement, challenged the Premier at an election in July of 1895, was defeated, stood for a suburban constituency in February of 1896, was defeated again, and died a broken man on 22 April.

Australia has proved unkind to her greatest servants. Macquarie left her a disappointed man to die unrewarded; Wentworth, the least unlucky, had to spend his old age at the other end of the world to avoid worse disappointment: Deakin, as we shall see, shattered himself in the Commonwealth's service and died many years before his death. So Parkes, probably the most naturally able statesman (and certainly the most unswervingly patriotic) Australia has used, passed from the stormy magnificence of his great premierships to a pitiful old age of petulant querulousness, and died the victim of cruel misfortune in both his public

new Convention should be elected by popular vote to revise the draft Constitution or make a fresh one. It was this direct public vote that won the final victory.

and his private life—for his second wife, most dearly loved and valiantly cherished, died during the disastrous election of 1895. For some years his memory was treasured only by a few ardent Federationists, and it was not till the accomplishment of Federation that he was again honoured for a moment as its creator. But as the lapse of years dulls the impression of his foibles and failings—and of both he had many—the real greatness of the man begins to stand out again. By sheer will-power and intensity of character he evolved from his own misfortunes the welfare of his fellow-men. Too careless of money for his own prosperity, he gave New South Wales many years of sound financial administration, choosing his instruments therefor with skilful care. Uneducated in his childhood, never competent as a man to express nobly in written words the ideas that seethed in his brain, he established for Australian children the bases of a sound education (if only his successors will administer his schools intelligently), and encouraged by all means within his power struggling writers of greater literary talent. "Temperamental," spasmodic, difficult to live with and to work under, he could in any real crisis summon from his temperament qualities essential to a leader—"the intellectual greed that absorbed new ideas and inchoate reforms from all quarters, the zeal that enabled him to carry through the reforms and impress the ideas on the public, the invincible pride that refused to acknowledge defeats, however severe"; and he will remain undisturbed in the memory of many coming generations as the great begetter of their schools, their national integrity, and their continent-wide Commonwealth.

ALFRED DEAKIN

WHEN Henry Parkes died in April 1896 he left the unfinished work of Federation to his friend, Edmund Barton, and his enemy, George Reid. Barton, who later figured as "the Grand Old Man of Australia" (a title awarded to him by the Sydney *Bulletin* mainly in order to annoy Reid), was handicapped by his natural indolence and his unattractiveness as a public speaker. His "propaganda" work for Federation was effected chiefly by inspiring younger enthusiasts to carry on a vigorous campaign from end to end of the populated districts; but he was also a majestic figurehead, a sort of battle-flag that the regiment of intellectuals carried proudly to victory. Reid was the exact opposite of all this. His figure, his voice, everything about him was comic; it never occurred to people to follow him—they came crowding about him, carrying him along with them, laughing, cheering, in high good humour with themselves and with him, and yet unconsciously moving in the direction he was choosing. The witnesses of such a movement, if they were not caught up in it, stood aside disgustedly or contemptuously, wondering at the "mountebank's" power to attract. It was inevitable that two such leaders should quarrel continuously, and between them should go near to wrecking the cause in which they were both supposed to be fighting—though for Barton it was a cause to be upheld on principle, to Reid it was a goal of doubtful value if attained, but one whose attaining might "dish" his political opponents and bring fame and high position to himself.

Parkes's real successor, therefore, was neither Barton

nor Reid, but a young man from the rival colony of Victoria, as polished as Parkes was crude, as altruistic as Reid was selfish, as exuberantly energetic as Barton was indolent. Hardly known outside his own colony until he became Prime Minister of the Commonwealth, perpetually misunderstood by the men who should have been standing behind him, and estimated at his true value by few except the men against whom political exigencies forced him to contend—he never willingly fought anyone—Alfred Deakin was probably the most efficient single influence in the Federation campaign, and certainly the greatest and most creative influence in the years of detailed organisation that followed the birth of Australia.

Born on 3 August, 1856, of an English (Northamptonshire) father and a Welsh mother in a Melbourne suburb, the child Alfred was a strange mixture of mischievous high spirits and almost extravagant dreaminess. His school life was a period of garrulous ringleadership among his mates, of routine lessons just well enough studied not to displease his masters beyond an affectionate patience. But the background of the school life, and the whole of the vacation life, was a total immersion in books and dreams. As soon as he was old enough, the alcoves of the Melbourne Public Library were his invariable holiday haunt; before he was fourteen he was soaked in *The Pilgrim's Progress, Robinson Crusoe, Gulliver's Travels,* and *The Arabian Nights,* passing then to Byron and Shelley and Keats, Wordsworth and Tennyson, tackling Carlyle at sixteen, Herbert Spencer at seventeen, Ruskin at eighteen. This may sound like a list of famous authors such as any young man might feel it his duty to study at least perfunctorily. No study that he cared for was perfunctory with Alfred Deakin. He read everything of each author that he could get at, and remembered almost everything. His memory was prodigious, only surpassed by his application; he was probably the only person in Australia, and one of a very few in the world, who read everything Wordsworth had written, prose and poetry alike. Moreover, as soon as he left school and was not compelled by outside pressure to study according to fixed methods, he brought all the bookish side of his life out into the open. He thrashed out Carlylean and Spencerian and Wordsworthian doctrines with a succession of friends, he joined debating clubs and spoke regularly, he wrote voluminously — fiction and lyrics and drama—and was not ashamed to abandon publicly views that he had thus tried out and found reason to distrust. At eighteen he was one of those "promising" young men of whom friends expect marvels, while cautious acquaintances with greater experience shake their wise heads.

Then of a sudden his inner life took a sharp curve. He was studying for the Bar, earning money the while sometimes by teaching at a private school, sometimes as bookkeeper in a printing and stationery business. But what really interested and absorbed him from eighteen to twenty-four was spiritualism. At twenty-one he published *A New Pilgrim's Progress*, dictated to him by the spirit of John Bunyan; next year he was made president of the Victorian Spiritualist Association. In spite of the ephemeral mediumship, however, he never really convinced himself that this new creed was sound, and in 1880–1 he diverged toward Swedenborgianism, which held his emotional interest for many years.

It is not of such material that statesmen are usually made, or even great politicians. Deakin was in need of severer discipline than he could obtain from legal studies or mystic religiosities. It came to him from an unexpected quarter—the press. Spiritualistic circles of those days included two remarkable brothers, David and George Syme. The biography of David Syme, one of the most nearly irresistible forces the colony of Victoria ever bowed under, has yet to be written impartially. The memories of his dour despotism, imposed by means of his fearless and wholly independent management of his newspaper, the *Age*, still oppress Victorian politics; the indelible stamp of his personality is still deep on all who were for any length of time in close contact with him. But for Deakin, he would have held his colony back from Federation, and there would have been no Commonwealth; but it was he who trained the young Deakin to control and direct energies that were consuming him, who forged the weapon that conquered even David Syme. In 1878 George Syme, a smaller man but a harder master, brought the young lawyer to his brother's office and had him set to leader-writing. The novice, who had hoped to be given space for academic matter, found his new task hard to understand, and was transferred to George's sphere, the *Age's* weekly *Leader*, where he was ordered to produce concise and intelligent summaries of each week's news for perusal by the country-folk who were the *Leader's* public. He was miserable; he was bullied almost unendurably by George; in the end David, who kept an eye on him, saw that the discipline was becoming too strenuous, and took him back on the *Age*. But the experience had been invaluable. For the first time in his life Deakin had been forced to consider the other man's point of view, to write not as he liked but as his readers could understand, to use the glittering weapon that was his mind in actual conflict and against human dullness and human indifference, as well as against opponents of his own class. The lesson once learnt, David Syme judiciously varied the work he needed with the work he liked, adapted his academic studies to political ends, taught him—as Jowett taught his best scholars—that the prime use of hard philosophical training is to provide leaders for a nation.

It may seem that in so brief a sketch of Deakin's life as this needs must be too much space has been devoted to his youth. But without an adequate account of the formative years the man would be incomprehensible. Abnormally literate for an Australian of his times, abnormally philosophic for a politician of any times, he developed from his boyish hobbies and their disciplined adolescence both the lasting success that attended his policies and the repeated failures that mar his personal career. Only with such a youthful history as background do the persistences and the vagaries of his middle life become intelligible.

His early political life may be treated briefly; it was of great interest to Victoria, but comparatively ineffective in relation to Australia. Syme plunged him in 1879 into a whirlpool of local legislative problems, centring on what the *Age* and its clientele considered the undue predominance of the Victorian Upper House. Elected as a supporter of Graham Berry, the Radical leader in Parliament, Deakin distinguished himself at first by a prompt resignation of his seat because the validity of the election had been challenged. His maiden speech, not quite a masterpiece because it was a thought too mannered and too erudite, he ended with a refusal to take any further part in debate until a new election should be held:

If I am the representative of the majority of the electors of West Bourke, I shall be returned again; if I am not their representative, I have no right to be here. . . . The honour of a seat in this House came to me unsolicited, and it shall leave me at least unsullied.

The gesture was characteristic of him. So, too, was

Berry's comment of Berry: "It's all very well for you—it puts you on a pinnacle; but what of the Party if you lose them a seat at this juncture?" He lost it, and was defeated again in February 1880, but returned at the head of the poll in July of the same year. Within a few weeks, and before he was twenty-four years old, he was offered the Attorney-Generalship by Berry. He refused at once; but for the next twenty years no Ministry was formed in Victoria without Deakin's being offered a post in it, though of the nine offers he accepted two only. For indeed his heart was not in the work; "I became a politician," he wrote afterwards, "from 1880 till 1890 by sheer force of circumstances rather than independent choice." In 1883 he followed Berry into a Coalition Cabinet; in 1886 he succeeded Berry as Liberal leader in a second Coalition Cabinet; after November 1890 he did not again administer a Victorian department. The greater part of the 1880–90 period he spent in silence, feeling himself still an apprentice even while in office. But during the decade he made two notable marks, one on Victorian, the other on Imperial history.

In 1880–2 a severe drought affected north-eastern Victoria, where a large number of settlers had recently been planted on land hitherto devoted to sheep-breeding. The Coalition Ministry of 1883 decided to investigate the effects of irrigation, found that the literature of the subject was meagre, and made Deakin chairman of a Commission with directions to study Californian systems. Within three months in the early part of 1885 he had investigated irrigation work in five American States, and compiled a report which was forthwith adopted by the Government of the United States as a student's textbook on the subject. In 1886 he carried through the Victorian legislature an Irrigation Act and several Water-Supply Acts which established district irrigation trusts in many areas of the Murray valley on its Victorian side; the most notable of these is Mildura, originally a private speculation (under Government supervision) of the brothers Chaffey. From this legislation practically all modern Australian irrigation systems have developed. It must be noted, however, that Deakin was still in the apprentice stage, and insufficiently acquainted with average human nature; unused to dealings with unscrupulous people, he forgot to insert in his legislation precautions against dishonesty or wilful negligence, and the misfeasances of district trusts soon saddled the Government with bad debts and disgusted many people with the whole irrigation policy. His work, therefore, brought Deakin as much discouragement as credit, and for a time revived his earlier reputation for dreaminess and unpracticality.

It was unlucky that the even more important and practical work which during these years he achieved in Imperial politics made no particular impression in Victoria. In 1887 he was chosen, with James Service and Graham Berry from the first (then extinct) coalition, to represent his colony at the Colonial Conference of that year. At the opening meeting, when delegates were vieing with each other in compliments to the British Government, Deakin promptly spoke his mind about the Colonial Office:

One has only to turn to the despatches which have passed between this country and the Australian colonies upon the subject of New Guinea and the New Hebrides, and to compare them with the despatches, published in the same Blue Book, taken from the White Book of the German Empire, and with extracts from despatches issued by the French Colonial Office, to notice the marked difference of tone. The despatches received from England, with reference to English activity in those seas, exhibited only the disdain and indifference with which English enterprise is treated in the Colonial Office. . . . We hope that from this time forward Colonial policy will be considered Imperial policy; that Colonial interests will be considered, and felt to be Imperial interests; that they will be carefully studied, and that, when once they are understood, they will be most determinedly upheld.

This attitude, in the London of 1887, was daring enough. Worse—from the official point of view—was to come. At a secret meeting of the Conference, called to consider the French claim to the New Hebrides, Lord Salisbury (then both Prime Minister and Minister for Foreign Affairs) took some trouble to explain to the ignorant visitors from Australia how valueless the islands were, and how stupid it was to endanger British relations with France by objecting to French annexation of the group. Several Australian delegates accepted this pronouncement, some with apologies for their own ignorance, others with submissive regret. Deakin alone made a fighting speech. He contested Lord Salisbury's facts, he criticised severely Lord Salisbury's logic; winding up a vehement speech,

The people of Victoria, at any rate [he said], will never be parties on any terms to the cession of the New Hebrides; Australians have made this question their own, and will for ever resist the humiliation of a surrender which would greatly weaken their confidence in the Empire.

The immediate results of this boldness surprised Deakin's colleagues. Lord Salisbury, recognising a fellow-statesman among the ruck of half-trained politicians whom he despised, accepted the rebuke with perfect good temper and acted at once on the information given him, instructing the ambassador at Paris to maintain to the full all British claims in the New Hebrides. Deakin himself was offered the K.C.M.G., and refused it—as he did all titles and decorations consistently throughout his life. Though the rest of his work at the Conference was inconspicuous, it was strenuous and valuable, and his personal position was marked by an important newspaper's dictum that

> Any views which he may in future express as the mouthpiece of Victoria will be sure to receive an amount of consideration, at the hands of English statesmen of the first rank, which has rarely before been accorded to any colonial public man.

In Australia these happenings were unknown for many years, and the Conference did little for Deakin's reputation. But the experience embedded deep in his mind one firm conviction. On Australian questions the delegates of the six Australian colonies had never been unanimous, and Australian interests had suffered thereby. Nothing serious could be achieved until Australia spoke in the councils of the Empire with a single voice. His master-motive from that time forth was the accomplishment of Federation.

Partly for this reason, partly because his position as joint head of a Coalition Ministry forced on him the responsibility for many political compromises every one of which was to his own soul both a torture and a breach of faith, Deakin decided to remove himself as quickly as possible from the sphere of Victorian party politics. When in 1890 the Coalition Ministry was defeated, he left office with a determination never to take it again except in a federated Australia. There was plenty of work awaiting him elsewhere; he had taken advantage of the visit to England to study irrigation in Italy and Egypt on the way home, and as soon as he was free of office the *Age* asked him to pursue similar studies in India. He spared two months for this visit, and constructed from it some excellent journalism; then he returned to Melbourne and sat down to the work of his life. To create Australia from the muddled contiguities of six ill-matched, querulous colonies—to make, if one may misquote Browning, from six dissonances "not a seventh sound, but a star"—

and to provide for the new nation organisations, policies and ideals that would befit a mighty state, were from this time forth his permanent objectives and his heart's desire.

The beginnings of the great Federation campaign have already been described in their association with Henry Parkes. Deakin first actively interfered in it when he persuaded Duncan Gillies to take part in the Melbourne Conference of 1890, and followed this up with a strong advocacy, at the Conference, of early and unfettered Federation. In the Convention of 1891 he took a subordinate but very active part, coming into the public view mainly as a champion of the "Lower" (popularly elected) House of the proposed legislature against the "Upper" House which was designed to protect the separate interests of the several colonies. The immediate issue, it will be remembered, was the amount of control over money Bills that might be allotted to the "Senate," and it was Deakin who procured the arrangement which still stands—that the Senate, though neither originating nor actually amending money Bills, may "suggest" amendments which the other House will consider. As between the six colonies and the new Australia he had for the time being no doubt, for his ideal was "a strong government upon the broadest popular basis, and with the amplest national power"; the exact division of powers troubled him little, and at one time he was ready to leave each colony its own Post Office, so long as the Federal Government had absolute control of defence and fiscal policies. In later life, when he found Labour likely to control Federal politics, he drifted back towards the maintenance of State sovereignty as a counterbalance; but in the nineties he would have readily accepted a constitution like that of the South African Union. Apart from the "suggestion" of Senate amendments his most noticeable achievement in

1891 was the part he took in naming the new Dominion. It was Parkes, always ready to envisage himself as a nineteenth-century Cromwell, who suggested "The Commonwealth"; it was Deakin who by persistent canvass of the delegates, as well as by zealous public advocacy, secured its adoption.

The Constitution devised in 1891 was a politicians' affair, as the Convention had been. When the Parliament of New South Wales shelved it, no other colonial legislature was interested enough to revive its discussion. Deakin, always impatient of political byways and anxious that Federation should be the spontaneous outgrowth of national feeling, determined to appeal directly to the electors. He turned to the Australian Natives' Association (which, in spite of its name, has always been a purely Victorian institution, branches in the other colonies having invariably degenerated into cliques of ineffective busybodies) and used it for intensive mission work throughout Victoria. "Mission" work is the right word, for he and his followers preached Federation as a religion rather than a policy. When by methods that have already been described the problem was again brought up for solution in 1895–6, the Victorian legislature was more or less critical of its implications, but the people of Victoria were wholeheartedly in favour of Federation; when after the Convention of 1897–8 the revised Constitution was submitted to popular vote, Victoria provided seventy per cent of the first Australian majority in its favour and sixty per cent of the second.[1] That was Deakin's work.

In the Convention of 1897–8, to which he was elected a Victorian representative by popular vote, he was again

[1] The actual figures are still more impressive. In the first vote the Victorian record was 100,520 against 22,099; in the second it was 152,653 against 9805.

rather a silent influence than a figure in the public eye. His chief work was the lubrication of the wheels, the appeasement of personal jealousies and political distrust among his fellow-members. It would be hard to point to any single provision of the Constitution as originating from him; it would be hard, too, to discover any important provision that went through without his personal aid. When the Convention dissolved, however, he sprang into prominence. David Syme had not been a convert, and inaugurated a campaign against the Constitution Bill as favouring New South Wales rather than Victoria; several of the Victorian representatives were ready to propagate this view, and it looked as if all the work were going for nothing. Deakin turned to the Australian Natives' Association, persuaded its governing body to reassert their pro-Federation views, and had his two principal Victorian opponents invited to a banquet the same evening. They made their speeches, full of lamentation and mourning and woe. Deakin, who had spent the day in vain attempts to convert Syme, sprang up as the last pessimist sat down, and made a speech that has been described as "his high-water mark as an orator"; we cannot from the poor press reports reconstruct it, but its effect was unmistakable—the banqueters pledged themselves *en masse* to the cause, the pessimists bowed before the storm, and Syme himself after a week's reflection swung his newspaper behind the orator and offered him its leading columns for his platform. One lion was still in the path. George Reid, never an ardent Federalist, had enticed his colony towards apostasy by demanding that Sydney should be made the Federal capital city. It was Deakin who devised the compromise that finally disarmed Reid—the proposal that the capital should be placed in New South Wales, at least one hundred miles from Sydney (this to placate Victorian jealousy), and should be surrounded by a block of Federal, not of New South Wales, territory.

One task remained before the Commonwealth could come into being. The Bill, approved in five colonies by a sixty per cent majority of the electors in each, must be passed by the Imperial Parliament. Barton—who had won Deakin's friendship during the long Australian campaign, and was to become rather his mouthpiece than his chief in the first Federal Ministry—was commissioned by the New South Wales Parliament to visit London as an adviser to the Imperial Government should alterations be proposed at Westminster, and his companions were Deakin from Victoria, Kingston from South Australia, Dickson from Queensland, and Fysh from Tasmania. The chief obstacle to the Parliament's unqualified assent—or rather to that of the Colonial Office, for Parliament would have accepted with docility whatever Joseph Chamberlain and the permanent officials chose to recommend—was the limitation of appeals to the Judicial Committee of the Privy Council. The original Bill made the new High Court of Australia the final authority on all cases involving constitutional questions. The Colonial Office insisted that in these as in all other cases a final appeal should lie to the Judicial Committee. Barton, always a little awed by Imperial officials (as he was to prove not long afterwards over the unfortunate Naval Agreement of 1902), might have yielded. Dickson, inspired (Heaven knows why!) by that great but spasmodic personality Samuel Griffith, at the moment Chief Justice of Queensland, was whole-heartedly for submission. Deakin and Kingston, supported sincerely but passively by Fysh, fought hard for the Bill as the five colonies had accepted it. Outsiders now joined in the dispute. The Agent-General for New Zealand—a colony which had taken no part in the debates of 1897-8—advocated publicly a postponement of the whole affair; a delegate from Western Australia, which had not accepted the Bill, but still might accept it, backed Dickson and the Colonial Office. In May the Bill was submitted to the House of Commons (as a schedule to a British Bill) with the obnoxious clause omitted. Then, at the last moment, Chamberlain relented and proposed a compromise whereby constitutional questions as between the Commonwealth and a State or between States should be left absolutely to the Australian High Court unless the Governments concerned agreed to appeal to the Judicial Committee. But legal questions of this kind were not likely —so the Australian public in those days believed—to involve the interests of the comparatively poor majority of citizens; the wealthier citizens and corporations, whose interests might be involved, distrusted the as yet non-existent Court a good deal and their colonial Governments much more; the Chamberlain compromise would not do. At last Griffith suggested that appeals on constitutional questions to the Judicial Committee might be allowed at the discretion of the High Court itself, and all parties—chiefly because they were sick of the whole subject and wanted Federation off their hands—accepted this solution. The Bill went through, and Australia became a nation. But it was to Deakin mainly, both as upholder of Australian rights and as conciliator in the negotiations (which Kingston had more than once almost broken off), that the success was due. Chamberlain sent him his personal thanks for the work accomplished, and years afterwards repeated that Deakin had been his most steadfast opponent and his best persuader.

Of the intrigues that beset the establishment of a Federal Administration there is no need to write here. No Ministry could have for long stood without Deakin, and the Barton

Ministry, which was actually the first, owed its life to him. Entering the new Parliament as member for the important mining and agricultural centre of Ballarat, and the Ministry as Attorney-General, he set himself to accomplish in eight years of strenuous but on the whole happy labour the biggest task of his life — the discovery and formulation of basic principles on which the whole Federal structure must be organised. The maintenance of a "White Australia," the building up of necessary industries by protective duties and bounties and their control by compulsory arbitration, the defence of Australia as an integral part of the British Empire both by organising the man-power already there and by introducing suitable immigrants to provide more man-power, the linking-up of the nation so defended with its fellow-nations and with the mother-country by frequent mutual consultations, by preferential tariffs, by sharing with Britain such Imperial burdens as could be allotted to a small, distant, energetic and versatile community—all these aims were constantly present to his vision, and every act of his public life was directed towards their ultimate attainment. They were not new, of course, not invented or first seen by him then. But he was the first to see them all as parts of one great policy, to interlink all endeavours towards each of them so that by the achievement of one all the others were brought nearer. Towards the end of his political career it became possible to write without a tinge of exaggeration:

It is almost impossible to over-state Mr. Deakin's dominance in matters of Federal policy. . . . It was always his policy that Parliament was endeavouring to carry out. Except the principle of compulsion in military training, which he accepted at first half-heartedly, the principles of all-important legislation during the whole period were of his preaching, and many of the more essential details were of his devising. . . . The Australian people, growing into a sober and determined manhood mainly through

the wisdom and forethought of Alfred Deakin's administration, have accepted in all essentials the national policy he framed.—
Quarterly Review, October 1911.

To justify these generalisations in detail would occupy here a disproportionate space and probably weary the reader instead of convincing him. But a summary of Deakin's actual legislative achievement may be permitted.

As Attorney-General in the Barton Ministry of 1901–3 he was responsible for the Immigration Restriction Act (the instrument of the White Australia policy) and its concomitant Pacific Labourers Act. The latter had little to do with White Australia, being concerned mainly with the suppression of recruiting in the Melanesian Islands (which had in past years created much scandal) and the return to their own homes of Kanakas who had been thus recruited for the Queensland sugar plantations.[1] In carrying the main (Immigration Restriction) Act through the legislature, it should be noted, Deakin had to fight hard against angry demands (not only from Labour members, but from such strong Conservatives as George Reid and William McMillan) for a direct prohibition of Asiatic, African and Polynesian immigration: he would himself have preferred this straightforward course, but felt bound to accept the Colonial Office view that discrimination avowedly on the ground of race or colour would unnecessarily offend both friendly Powers and fellow-subjects within the Empire.

In the session of 1903 Deakin's chief share was his

[1] The employment of white labour on the canefields which this Act made necessary did not bring about the cane-growers' ruin, as had been prophesied. A leading grower admitted some years afterwards that the industry had greatly benefited by the change; he personally regretted it, because it removed the Kanakas from the Christian influences that had surrounded them in Queensland, and necessitated the dispatch of more missionaries to the islands.

Judiciary Act, a masterpiece acknowledged by all both in construction and in the speeches with which he advocated it. The most important Bill of the session, Kingston's Arbitration Bill, was dropped when Kingston resigned; in the consequent reorganisation of the Ministry Deakin became Prime Minister, and in the session of 1904 remodelled the Bill to serve as a basis for the systematic control of industrial conditions which he was already devising. Having caused the fall of two Ministries (one of them Deakin's), the Bill passed into law at the year's end in the shape Deakin had devised for it, and it was many years before his basic principles were tampered with.

Soon after the session of 1905 opened he was in office again, and the legislation of the next three years was entirely his. In 1905 he improved the Immigration Restriction Act, did his best to restore honesty to trade by Acts dealing with trade descriptions and secret commissions, and obtained legislative sanction for the taking over of British New Guinea (since known as Papua) from Britain. In 1906 he initiated legislation for the suppression of "dumping" and of the misuse of monopolistic powers by private companies, and for safeguarding consumers and employees against any manufacturer who might seek to take advantage of the protection given him by a high tariff; his device was to facilitate in advance the lowering of protective duties on goods sold in Australia at an exorbitant price, and the imposition of excise duties on goods produced under objectionable labour conditions. Practically all this legislation, however, was pronounced unconstitutional by the High Court, and its chief result was to establish Deakin's aims as aims that must some day be attained by other means. The session of 1907-8, hampered to begin with by the Prime Minister's illness after a too strenuous Imperial Conference that is dealt with below, proved unexpectedly fruitful. A Federal Old Age Pensions Act was passed, and one authorising the construction of the railway that connects Western Australia by land with the eastern States—a vital need of genuine Federation—and one granting bounties for the establishment of new or infant industries such as cotton- and tobacco-growing. But the chief achievement was a new tariff, based entirely on Deakin's Imperialistic desires, and combining better protection for genuinely Australian industries with a preferential tariff for British manufactures. The imperfections of the scheme were many, but the principles involved in it are permanent, and lie at the back of all tariffs since constructed; Australia was to strengthen her position as a pillar of the Empire (a) by making herself as self-supporting as possible in respect of necessities, (b) by taking from British factories as much as possible of her other requirements. An even more important event, which was to bear ripe fruit under other auspices, was Deakin's exposition in December 1907 of his considered proposals for Australian defence. On the naval side these proposals were afterwards much altered in detail, but his principles remained and remain: Australia must maintain, man, and own a squadron of warships that would at the same time be part of the Imperial Navy, with Imperial standards of discipline and training, the officers and men being . . . in every other respect indistinguishable from the men in the Imperial squadrons here or elsewhere.

The military scheme contemplated universal service and the requisite training without actual conscription—a very Deakinesque conception; this was subsequently altered by the introduction of compulsory training, but otherwise exists to-day much as he foreshadowed it.

It was June of 1908 before the tariff was put through, and

in the following session Deakin's career as an independent politician came to an end. Noting briefly that his programme for that session included Bills formulating his defence proposals, acquiring the Northern Territory from South Australia, establishing an iron industry by means of bounties, encouraging immigration, and altering the Constitution so as to legalise the 1906 Acts for regulating prices and wages through the tariff—a sufficiently comprehensive and notable list—we must turn back to consider the conditions under which this Moses of the Commonwealth had achieved his work.

One might well imagine that he had been supported for years by a strong majority in Parliament. Far from it. Never from the moment in 1903 when he became Prime Minister had he any majority at all. Nor, for that matter, had anyone else until in 1910 the electors gave one to Labour. The Parliaments with which Deakin had to work were constructed on what he, disparagingly, called the "three elevens" system; there were always three independent bodies in them, and sometimes four. For a two-party system, such as British parliamentarianism demands for its success, can be fashioned only when a single political issue so far dominates all the rest that men are willing to postpone their other predilections to the attainment of that one. Free Trade was such an issue in the 1840's, Home Rule for Ireland in the 1880's; in Australia Free Trade had a long reign, which ended for all practical purposes with the first Federal Parliament. Before that time the leaders of "Labour," remembering how their forces had been split in New South Wales by the intrusion of fiscal issues among their own industrial policies, had ordained that a member's fiscal opinions were his own, and had nothing to do with his Labour pledges; thenceforth Labour maintained a definite and permanent position among

Federal parties, and, until it was strong enough to stand by itself, made its motto "Support in return for concessions" —a motto which was speedily adopted by the other parties also. Those other parties were, roughly speaking, the reactionary and the progressive party (the epithets are used literally, not with any implied slur on either); the party that distrusted all new developments—Deakin once described its platform as "a necklace of negatives"—and the party that was willing to experiment.

So in 1904, when he first faced a legislature elected under his own leadership, Deakin found himself at the head of twenty-seven supporters, with twenty-four Labour members on the cross-benches and twenty-four followers of George Reid in direct opposition. As his Arbitration Bill in one clause at least ran counter to Labour wishes, he was soon driven from office and succeeded by the Labour leader, who obtained temporary support from most of Deakin's followers. Four months later Reid won over enough Deakinites (including the leader himself) to defeat Watson, and took office with two prominent Deakinites in his Ministry and enough at his back to give him a majority of one. The position was unstable beyond description, though Reid retained office (mainly in recess) for almost eleven months; when by agreement with Labour Deakin at last put an end to it, he said truthfully: "I think we shall all welcome the disappearance of a Ministry that has neither achievement in the past, policy in the present, nor prospects in the future, to justify its existence."

For the next three years, as we have seen, Deakin was in power to the extent that he passed such Acts as he chose. For eighteen months he worked with the support of Labour's twenty-four and most of his own original twenty-seven— some had fallen away to Reid; at the elections of December

1906, his personal following was reduced to seventeen, Labour numbering twenty-six and the reactionaries thirty-two—before the end of the Parliament, however, fission had converted this body into two, one headed as before by Reid, the other leaderless but vaguely guided by John Forrest and W. H. Irvine. Yet Deakin, at the head of less than a quarter of the House, used it to carry out his own policies. The result was so surprising that the Opposition press repeatedly accused him of pandering to Labour to maintain himself in office. That was not Labour's opinion. "The Government," said a Labour senator, "have done everything they could to show that they have no desire to consult, satisfy, or in any way conciliate the Labour Party. . . . I might almost say that in regard to administration the Government have despised the Labour Party." Deakin's one secret—at once his strength as a statesman and his vital defect as a party leader—was that he cared for nothing but his policies, and above all for his country. "Whether you vote Yes or No," he said at one election, "provided you vote as Australians, we shall not have anything to complain of." His temporary alliance with Reid in 1904–5, his longer alliance with Labour in 1905–8, his fatal "fusion" with the anti-Labour party in 1909–10, were all founded on the acceptance by his would-be allies of his programme; no other conditions satisfied him. And when in 1910–12 the Fisher Ministry, at last provided by the electors with a clear majority, began to carry through its own measures, it was for the most part his policy that it placed on the statute-book; when he as leader of the then Opposition attacked Fisher's proposals, the best answer was usually to be found in quotations from his own earlier speeches.

Before we discuss the ruinous error which in 1909 lost him his independence and his leadership, the efficient cause

Alfred Deakin 119

of the error—which was at the same time the culmination of his career as an Imperial statesman—falls to be considered. In 1907, twenty years after the first Colonial Conference, was summoned the fourth and last of those strange diets, already in process of transformation to an Imperial Council. Deakin, undisputed spokesman of a united Australia (for his proposals were accepted without opposition before he left for England by resolution of the Federal Parliament), hoped in the full fervour of his enthusiasm for the Empire to range against the known *laissez-faire* predilections of the British (the Campbell-Bannerman) Ministry a united band of colonial Prime Ministers proffering the following programme: An Imperial Council, with its own permanent secretariat; preferential tariffs acting mutually between Britain and her colonies; a new naval policy, giving the colonies more active work and seats on an Imperial Defence Council; and reforms in the Colonial Office that would allow its permanent officials to gain some personal knowledge of the territories they were supposed to supervise. Reaching London early, he drew to his side at once Dr. Jameson from the Cape Colony, Sir Joseph Ward from New Zealand, and Mr. Moor from Natal. All depended on Sir Wilfrid Laurier. He arrived at the last moment, was caught up from the train-side by Winston Churchill (then Under-Secretary for the Colonies), and carried off to the Colonial Office—from which he emerged some hours later its firm ally. In view of the British Ministry's attitude towards all colonial desires, this breach in the colonial phalanx was fatal to Deakin's hopes. Nevertheless he fought gallantly, secured a little more publicity for the proceedings of the Conference than Lord Elgin was willing to grant, and obtained a more definite and more imposing status for the self-governing colonies (henceforth called "Dominions"); but his endeavour to provide them with a permanent instrument in London, a secretariat appointed by the several Dominions to keep the British Prime Minister in direct touch with their Governments, was scouted—Campbell-Bannerman refused to take Dominion affairs directly under his supervision, and the secretariat which the Colonial Office set up inside its own mechanism was staffed by clerks ignorant of the outside Empire and was presided over by a German. When the Office notified Deakin formally of the establishment of this hybrid, he minuted a reply that the affair had no interest for Australia.

With respect to preferential tariffs also he received a not unexpected rebuff. But the British rejection of his proposals was aggravated by a miserably inadequate official report of his speeches in Conference. He determined forthwith to appeal to the British public, and entered on a campaign of public speaking unparalleled in political history except, perhaps, by the Midlothian campaign of W. E. Gladstone. Preferential trade was his immediate text; the greater vision which he preached was that of an Imperial organism in which every part aided and was aided by the rest, nourished by "state action systematically directed towards the development of every means of binding our peoples together." For six weeks he maintained an output of nervous energy that might, if conserved, have kept him alive and dominant in Australia to-day; he shirked nothing, neither the Conference debates nor the public speeches nor the press interviews nor the mass of routine business that must follow an Australian Prime Minister across the world. He came back to Melbourne a broken man.

The breakdown was not at once apparent, even to himself. Thanks to the long tariff debates of 1907–8 he was able to reserve himself for the few bigger issues, and (as has been already noted) to promulgate at the end of 1907 his important defence schemes. But during 1908 his grip was relaxing, and this was to some extent the cause of the Labour revolt that in September of that year turned him out of office. Retiring to the corner benches, he at first supported the Fisher Ministry, but soon grew impatient with its guiding mechanism, the "Caucus," and suffered himself to be drawn towards an alliance with the party—in whose leadership Joseph Cook had succeeded George Reid—against which he had fought for seven years out of the Commonwealth's eight. On his usual terms—complete acceptance of his policies—he took the leadership of an unnatural "Fusion" in which he and Cook shared the Cabinet equally. Summoning the remains of his powers, he marked this last term of office by two great achievements—the carrying of his scheme for the creation of an Australian navy, and the settlement with the State Premiers of the contribution to be made by the Commonwealth in aid of their finances; but both were marred in detail, partly by the hampering influence of his new associates, partly by his own increasing infirmness of purpose. It was with much personal relief, though with intense surprise, that in April 1910 he found his Fusion emphatically rejected at the polls, and himself within an inch of defeat in his own constituency.

From that time forth he began to retire within himself. The Fusion's year had degraded him in his own eyes. Under pressure from men whom he knew to be his enemies he had in a dozen ways gone back on his cherished resolutions, had given the High Commissionership to an ex-politician, had resorted to borrowing for defence works and ships, had quarrelled with his most steadfast friends. Already in 1910 he could write: "My public career is over, and the sooner it ends the better for me." Two years of nominal leadership of an Opposition that in the main distrusted and disliked him (it was a new experience to be disliked by his followers), embittered by the constant pinpricks of a reactionary press that took every occasion to belittle him, completed the ruin. In 1912 he complained of loss of memory, "breakdown in faculty and in health, in brain and digestion. . . . I have at last learned what it is to feel a wreck"; at the end of the year he left politics altogether, and hoped to recover in quietude a little of his lost brain-power. It was too late. At the beginning of the war, urged by his old rival and colleague, Joseph Cook, he made one more attempt to do a little non-political work for Australia; for various now unimportant reasons this also failed, and the rest of his life— he did not die till 1919—was spent in the bosom of his family, and in almost complete mental solitude. The announcement on 8 October of that year that he had died the night before was accepted as the happy release of a great man long since shattered by his own greatness.

Toiling through the long catalogue of his achievements, one is perhaps inclined to lose sight of the man himself. Yet he was a finer spirit than any achievement could display; possibly the mere fact of his participation in public life was more valuable to Australia than any other result of his career. This is high praise, and is so meant. If it should be discounted as coming from a friend — and, indeed, I prize that friendship above all others I have formed—take the evidence of his biographer, Walter Murdoch, writing in Australia amid Deakin's lifelong associates:

> He was a man for whom life came to mean nothing if not an opportunity of service. . . . He loved Australia with a fervent love; but he looked beyond her bounds, and, seeing her fate linked indissolubly with the fate of the Empire, he was a passionate Imperialist. And he looked beyond the Empire, and saw the human race; he believed that in serving the cause of the Empire he was serving humanity. Finally, he believed that in serving man he

was serving God; and the service of God was for him the supreme purpose of life.

Such a man could not move among men less noble without imparting to them a trace of his nobility; such a man in high office, directing policies or controlling administrators, left to the Commonwealth not only a legacy of great objectives and wise counsel but a tradition of honourable dealing and unselfish zeal for the public welfare.

His most serious defect was, no doubt, the immediate consequence of his finest quality. Eager to serve Australia, and the Empire, and humanity, he sometimes forgot the present in contemplating the future. His vision was too telescopic to see always clearly what was under his feet. Moreover, he had an intense dislike for using compulsion, and a fervid belief in the inevitable triumph of reason, no matter how irrational and obtuse his opponents might show themselves. Hot with anger at some State Premier's folly, he would reflect a moment later that sooner or later the fellow surely must see reason; and, time being in no sense of the essence of any contract of his—for he was thinking in terms of the distant future—he would let the subject drop and hope against hope to convince the recalcitrant before it was too late to benefit posterity.

Yet we shall understand him ill if we think of him only as a public and political leader. Out of office—indeed, out of office hours—he was a splendid and inspiring influence, a charming host, a perfect friend. You could not know him and not be his friend.

It was impossible [writes Walter Murdoch] to spend a dull moment in his company. I think of him always as radiant with vivacity. Though he was middle-aged when I came to know him, I cannot think of him as other than young and ardent; and I have seen middle-aged men grow young again when they were with him.

The wide reading, the cultural interests, that marked his youth stayed with him to the end of his public career. When in the early days of the Commonwealth he bore on his shoulders a weight of ministerial cares — for it was his peculiar task to spur on his chief, Edmund Barton, and rein back his colleague, Charles Kingston, apart from his own responsibilities — he walked every morning more than a mile across open parks from home to office, discussing French literature or German philosophy as though he had no other interests in the world. During his Prime Ministership, a political pronouncement or discussion of high importance once ended, he passed on without an effort to talk, as one who was constantly studying it, of the development of European dramatic art or the implications of a new geographical discovery. His speeches, too, were marked by their clarity of style and their freedom from colloquial lapses. I heard him deliver an impromptu address (the subject was altered at the last moment, so that he could not have prepared it) before an audience of delegates from the great universities of the world, which, reported exactly as it was spoken, was a piece of accurate and well-phrased literature. Careless critics sometimes called him verbose because he spoke at length, but every word was needed to expound clearly his wealth of ideas, and every idea fitted exactly into its place in the exposition of his policy or his theme.

Enough has been said. If the reader has not by now discovered how fine, how lovable, how great a personality moulded the Commonwealth in its childhood, it is my fault, not Alfred Deakin's. Utterly unselfish, utterly patriotic, he was the friend of everyone who strove after straightforward and honourable dealing. And Australia may count herself fortunate beyond most nations if within this century she discovers for her service such another Australian.

SOME PIONEERS

JAN CARSTENSZOON

ABOUT the first discovery of Australia by Europeans volumes of controversy have been compiled and historical reputations have been lost and gained. A bold American professor has nominated Odysseus for the honours due to the pioneer (going so far as to publish a map that shows Australia as the Greeks' Hades, but tactfully omits the boundaries which must have separated Elysium from Tartarus); it is interesting to note that Odysseus was a prehistoric John Macarthur, and disembarked sheep on the underworld coast. If we discard Homer as a witness, at any rate Lucian knew something about kangaroos—they "use their bellies for pockets . . . they are all shaggy and hairy inside, so that the children enter them when it grows cold." The Ptolemaic geography, unfortunately, discouraged antipodes, and the existence of Australia—except as a mysterious strip of land beyond the Indian Ocean, with Fish-eaters at one end of it and Man-eaters at the other—was forgotten until Marco Polo's amanuensis went to sleep one summer afternoon and dreamt that Siam and Singapore were somewhere south of Java. That mistake produced a crop of fantastic maps on which enterprising students have founded discovery claims for Portugal and France; readers interested in such divagations will find the whole subject authoritatively treated of in G. Arnold Wood's *Discovery of Australia*.

In the orgy of inventiveness which has beset this problem it is perhaps not astonishing that hardly anyone knows even the name of the first European visitor whose account of his visit is still extant. The usual summary of early Australian history mentions the voyage of a small Dutch yacht, the *Duyfken* (the name is as often as not wrongly spelt) to the Gulf of Carpentaria; then reference is made to Torres, who certainly wriggled his way through the islands of Torres Straits, and as certainly was never within fifty miles of Australia; then attention is diverted to Dutch discoveries along the western coast, and the wreck of Pelsart's *Batavia*, and the magical name of Tasman—who was a bold navigator, but a coward ashore and a bully everywhere. Occasionally a summariser with plenty of space at his disposal adds a casual mention of the ships *Pera* and *Arnhem*, which discovered Arnhem Land in the Northern Territory, and whose captain, Carstensz by name (but they rarely name him), was massacred by Papuans on the outward voyage.

It happens, however, that Carstensz (or Carstenszoon—the extra "z" in Dutch names is merely an abbreviation for "son") was not massacred by Papuans or by anyone else. On the contrary, he explored carefully the whole length of the eastern shores of the Gulf of Carpentaria, came within an ace of discovering the strait that leads to the continent's eastern coast (if he had discovered it, Australia would have been partitioned among the European nations a hundred years before Cook's time), and left behind him both an elaborate journal of his voyage and a chart of the gulf's eastern coast that includes details not to be found on more recent maps. One may scarcely call him a "builder" of Australia, but he was assuredly one of the earliest and most assiduous surveyors of its site.

Of Carstensz himself we know nothing but what his journal tells us; the Dutch authorities of those days took great care not to betray much personal interest in the men they employed. But a summary of the work of his one known predecessor will be useful. The authorities at Batavia

Jan Carstenszoon

seem to have maintained a yacht, the *Duyfken*, for purposes of exploration, and on 28 November, 1605, dispatched her in charge of Willem Jansz from Bantam in Java to explore the regions east of Ceram. Charts of that area were vague, mainly dotted over with names of inlets that might be river-mouths on a continent or straits between islands; Spanish voyagers from Mexico seemed to have made sure of the northern coast of a long island—New Guinea—along which they had sailed while searching for the Spice Islands, but what record there was of its southern coast showed only a scattered archipelago. Jansz returned the next year with rough charts of a coast-line, not continuous, that stretched south-east from 5° S. lat. to nearly 14° S. lat., land being still visible beyond that. The *Duyfken*, however, had run short of provisions thereabouts, and Jansz marked "Keer Weer" (Turn back) on his chart[1] and made back to Bantam. His report is not now to be found, but it was extant for at least twenty years after his return; quotations from it are not encouraging—he had come into collision with "savage, cruel, black barbarians," and had lost some of his crew in fights. The Council at Batavia pondered the matter for another ten years. In 1616 they resolved to try

[1] This note of his terminal point has given later map-makers a great deal of trouble. In the first place, the Batavian Council of 1643 quoted it as "Cape Keer-weer," and along that stretch of coast there is nothing resembling a cape. Matthew Flinders, most punctilious of explorers, carefully inserted the name on his chart of the Gulf of Carpentaria, but he could not create a cape to fit it. In the second place, there are several other Keer-weers. Carstensz mentioned two—one in about 7° S. lat. on the coast of New Guinea, where the shore-line takes a sudden bend backwards, the other at his own terminal point in the gulf, about 17° 30′ S. lat.; and some unknown Dutch navigator put another on the coast-line of Celebes.

again, and left it at that; in 1622 they went so far as to compile instructions for an expedition, but that lapsed. While they were hesitating, Governor Van Speult of Amboyna forced their hand. He was a brutal man with foreigners— he carried through the "Amboyna massacre" that for a hundred years embittered the English beyond measure against the Dutch, but successfully warned our East India Company off Malaysian soil. Still, he was a patriotic Hollander, and even while he was killing and torturing Englishmen had time to fit out the yachts *Pera* and *Aernem* (or *Arnhem*) and to put them in charge of Jan Carstensz for a new voyage of discovery. Speult's main instructions were that Carstensz should repeat with scrupulous care, and extend if possible, the explorations of the *Duyfken*, reporting what prospects of trade or of exploitation there might be, and investigating the religion, social habits, and political institutions of all tribes or nations he might come across.

On 21 January, 1623, Carstensz left Amboyna with Jansz's chart (and maybe his journal too) as his only guide into the unknown. Cutting across from the Aru Islands to the coast of New Guinea, the adventurers on 11 February landed in 4° 20' S. lat. and came into conflict with some Papuans; ten Dutchmen were killed, and the master of the *Aernem* was fatally wounded, and died next day. This was a blow to Carstensz, for neither the new master nor the *Aernem's* pilot liked the work, and on more than one occasion afterwards the *Pera* had to wait for, or even to go back for, her reluctant companion. Progress was irritatingly slow. Near False Cape—where on 12 March they had another encounter with Papuans—they took a week to go twenty miles; on the 30th they found themselves hopelessly enmeshed in shallows that might neither be sailed over nor be waded across. On the 31st they came to a notable resolution—they would back out of the shallows as far as might be necessary westwards, and then strike directly south across open sea to about 16° S. lat.[1] and work back northwards from that point along the coast. While they were about it, they resolved also that the coast they had already skirted between 4° S. and 9° S. was unbroken, and should be marked on their chart as "Western End of New Guinea," and that the shallows which were blocking them should be named "Drooge Bocht" (Shallow Bight). They were stupendously democratic, these old Dutch voyagers, and put everything to the vote.

On 4 April they "managed with extreme difficulty and great peril to get again out of the shallows aforesaid, into which we had sailed as into a trap, between them and the land, for which happy deliverance God be praised." For eight days they made south across open sea, and on the 12th sighted for the first time the actual coast of Australia somewhere near Port Musgrave. Three days later Carstensz sent a man ashore, who saw aborigines in the distance but could not get into touch with them. On the 17th another landing was made—somewhere near the Mitchell River—where Carstensz noted "flat, fine country with few trees, and a good soil for planting and sowing, but so far as we could observe utterly destitute of fresh water." Next day they at last came into contact with the blacks, who in hair and figure, thought Carstensz, resembled the blacks of the Coromandel Coast—an acute observation, seeing that their nearest relatives, according to present-day theories, are the Dravidian tribes of Southern India. The aborigines were quite fearless, and one regrets to say that Carstensz took

[1] This implies possession of Jansz's chart; only from his indication could they foresee that there would be any shore-line in 16° S. to strike.

advantage of this to kidnap one of them—apparently in accordance with his instructions, since he afterwards told the Council that, if it needed more detailed information than he could give, it might question the native whom he had brought home for that purpose. The immediate result, however, was that the blacks on the 19th became decidedly hostile and attacked landing-parties, so that one of them had to be shot.

Still going south, on the 24th the ships found themselves in 17° 8′ S. lat., and began to think about return. Near the mouth of a stream, which by the usual resolution they named "Staten Revier,"[1] they put up a tablet recording their arrival:

Anno 1623 on the 24th of April there arrived here two yachts on behalf of their High Mightinesses the States-General.

Note the care taken not to claim any credit even for the ships; all must go to the States-General.

On the 26th the two vessels began the homeward voyage, but quarrels broke out at once. Carstensz's intention, formulated in the resolution of 31 March and repeated on 24 April, was to devote this part of the voyage to a close inspection of the coast previously untouched, in the hope of evading the Drooge Bocht and finding a way through where Jansz's chart vaguely indicated one. But the *Aernem's* master and crew were of a different opinion. They wanted to go home by the shortest possible route; and home they went. On the 27th, Carstensz records, the *Aernem* "on purpose and with malice prepense cut away from us against

[1] This was not the present Staaten River, but probably a mouth of the Gilbert. The names now current along the gulf coast were put there by Matthew Flinders, who worked conscientiously from Tasman's not very accurate chart, and made many incorrect identifications.

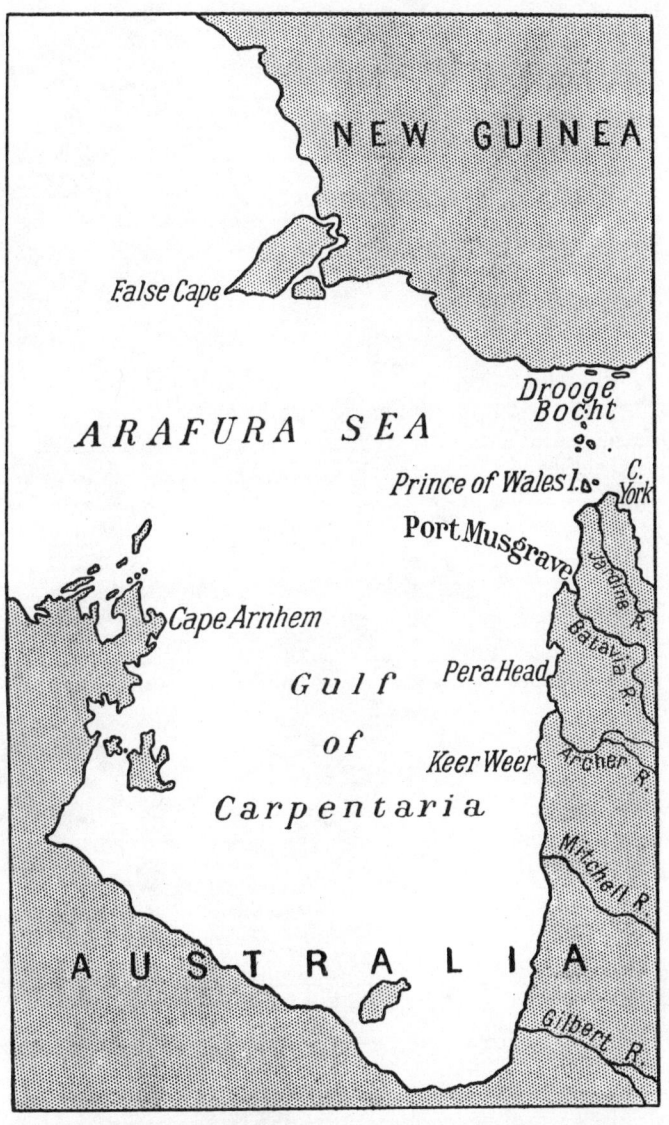

MAP OF THE COASTLINE OF NEW GUINEA AND NORTHERN
AUSTRALIA, TO ILLUSTRATE CARSTENSZOON'S VOYAGE

Jan Carstenszoon

her instructions and our resolution, and seems to have set her course for Aru, to have a good time of it there."[1] On that day, and for four days more, the *Pera's* men landed in search of water, but it was not until 1 May that they procured any, and then only by digging pits into which it filtered. By this time Carstensz was entirely disillusioned about his chances of exploiting the new discoveries. "We have not seen," says his journal, "one fruit-bearing tree, nor anything that man could make use of; there are no mountains or even hills, so that it may be safely concluded that the land contains no metals, nor yields any precious woods, such as sandal-wood, aloes or columba; in our judgment this is the most arid and barren region that could be found anywhere on the earth. The inhabitants, too, are the most wretched and poorest creatures that I have ever seen in my age or time."

On the 8th, near the mouth of the Archer River (which they named the "Coen") another blackfellow was captured for the Council—but Carstensz was less hopeful about his usefulness:

> We cannot, however, give any account of their customs and ceremonies, nor did we learn anything about the thickness of the population, since we had few or no opportunities for enquiring into these matters. Meanwhile I hope that, with God's help, Your Worships will in time get information touching these points from the black we have captured.

---

[1] Carstensz was unjust. She did not want a good time anywhere but at home. On 14 May she sailed into Banda Harbour, very sorry for herself, with a broken rudder, having been all but wrecked on what she called "Arnhem and Speult Islands"—really the north-eastern corner of the Northern Territory. It must be noted that the Instructions given to Tasman, so often quoted as indubitable evidence with regard to early Dutch discoveries, are inaccurate here, and probably in other places.

K

Jan Carstenszoon

They made several days' stay at the Archer mouth, and Carstensz took the opportunity to make a formal report on the newly found land. It repeats a little that he had already written, but is worth quoting *in extenso* as the first considered judgment of an Australian land area by a thoughtful European:

The land between 13° and 17° 8' is a barren and arid tract without any fruit-trees, producing nothing fit for the use of man. It is low-lying and flat, without hills or mountains, and in many places overgrown with brushwood and stunted wild trees. It has not much fresh water, and what little there is has to be collected in pits dug for the purpose; there is an utter absence of bays or inlets, except a few bights not sheltered from the sea-wind. It extends mainly N. by E. and S. by W., with shallows all along the coast, with a clayey and sandy bottom; it has numerous salt rivers extending into the interior, across which the natives convey their wives and children on dry logs or tree-boughs.

The natives are in general utter barbarians, all resembling each other in shape and features, coal-black, and with twisted nets wound round their heads and necks for keeping their food in; so far as we could make out, they chiefly live on certain ill-smelling roots which they dig out of the earth. We infer that during the eastern monsoon they live mainly on the beach, since we have there seen numerous small huts made of dry grass. We also saw great numbers of dogs, herons, and curlews, and other wild fowl, together with plenty of excellent fish easily caught with a seine-net. They are quite unacquainted with gold, silver, tin, iron, lead, and copper; nor do they know anything about nutmegs, cloves, and pepper, all of which spices we repeatedly showed them without their evincing any signs of recognising or valuing the same. From all which, together with the rest of our observations, it may safely be concluded that they are poor and abject wretches, caring mainly for bits of iron and strings of beads.

It is an excellent summary—of the district; it might be written to-day. As long as Australia was approached only along its northern and western shores, it remained safe from

European colonisation. One can but wonder that, after so comprehensive a curse, the authorities at Batavia ever gave the region another thought; but, as we shall see, Tasman, the next voyager they sent there, was given an entirely different errand, and failed in it through sheer cowardice.

On 9 May the *Pera* reached what is now Pera Head, the first sign of cliffs along the coast; it is an important landmark in the voyage, because the exact description of the head and of the large bay north of it for the first time gives us a definite identifiable point. Carstensz's observed latitude is only 20′ out (12° 33′ instead of 12° 53′), and from that noted error we can correct his other observations and identify other landing-places on his route. During the afternoon of the 11th they passed another landmark, "a large river which the men of the *Duyfken* went up in 1606, and where one of them was killed by the arrows of the blacks." Carstensz named the stream "Carpentier River," but the name was soon afterwards, for reasons unknown, altered to "Batavia." Just north of its mouth on the 12th they had another collision with the natives, wounded and captured a black, and on him found a piece of metal that had come from the *Duyfken*; it was noticed, too, that these blacks seemed to know the effect of musket-fire. On the 12th they anchored near the Van Speult River (not shown on modern maps —thank Heaven, the torturer's name has not been left on the map of Australia!) and on the 14th rounded a point of land and discovered "a fine fresh-water river" to which they gave no name; it is now the Jardine. Behind it the land was high and hilly, in front reefs guarded a sandy beach. What follows Carstensz shall relate himself:

> Towards evening we were about a mile from three islets, of which the southernmost was the largest; five miles, at a guess, farther north we saw mountainous country, which could not be

reached on account of the shallows. In almost every direction in which soundings were taken we found very slight depth, and for a long time sailed in 5, 4, 3, 2½, 2, 1½ fathoms and even less. At last we had to anchor in 1½ fathoms, but after sunset sent out the pinnace, which a long way south-west of the yacht found deeper water—2, 3, and 4½ fathoms. Blithely, therefore, we sailed the yacht in that direction, and cast anchor in 8½ fathoms, thanking God Almighty for His inexpressible mercy and tender heartedness.

Next day the wind was south-east, and return was impossible. They let the *Pera* run west, found the water shallowing again, and altered her course to south-west, which brought them into six fathoms but out of sight of land. Shallows, reefs, banks, and the easterly wind, a council decided, were too many dangers all at once; they had better go home and report what they had found, and leave it to others to investigate farther. On 8 June they reached Amboyna.

Why elaborate this futile departure from a land they had found so uninviting? Because the events of that 14 May were all-important in Australian history. When Carstensz turned his back on the Jardine and the hills behind it, he left the road clear for James Cook. On that 14th he was lying actually in the mouth of Endeavour Strait; the mountainous country northwards was Prince of Wales Island, Cape York was only twenty miles away. Within his reach—but for one obstacle—was the long-coveted gate to the South Seas, to the fertile lands of Eastern Australia, to a new Dutch colonial empire. But . . . the *Pera* was alone, and her crew was weary, and the land he had already seen was barren, and the shallows—no one aboard the yacht had forgotten their experience in early April, and it is quite possible that the crew would have mutinied if Carstensz had proposed to repeat it. Above all, there was the decisive obstacle, the south-east trade-wind.

One sometimes thinks that Australians should erect on

the most conspicuous position available a monument to the south-east trades. It is they that preserved the continent to become British. The one coast-line that invites visitors to stay and to explore it is the eastern; from Cape York west-about to Cape Catastrophe in South Australia there are very few stretches that lure the stray mariner inland, and these were somehow missed by Dutch and English alike until after Cook's time. But the eastern coast, once discovered, demanded colonisation; and from that part of the continent explorers were repeatedly driven by the south-east trades. Spaniards came across the Pacific from Mexico or Peru or Magellan Straits; wherever they started on the eastern side of the Pacific, the trades edged them north-westwards as they traversed it, and led them to the New Hebrides and the Solomons and New Guinea, but never to Australia. Torres in 1606 deliberately drove south-west across the trades to 21° S. lat., but then gave it up and let them take him back to New Guinea. Carstensz was blocked by them in the very mouth of the strait; his clumsy "yacht," barely able to maintain a five-knot speed with a favouring breeze, was helpless against their steady pressure. When in 1636 Gerrit Thomasz Pool was ordered to re-visit the gulf and correct Carstensz's observations, and Pool himself was killed by Papuans on the way, his successor, Pieter Pieterszoon, tried to reach his destination direct from the Aru group, but was held up by "the east and south-east winds blowing constantly with great vehemence and hollow seas." What Tasman did no man knows, but it is charitable to believe that the same obstacle had something to do with his failure. Last of all the Englishman William Dampier, deliberately seeking the eastern coast by way of northern New Guinea and New Britain, mistakenly steered too far round the latter island into Dampier Strait, and when he began to turn south again found the obstinate trades against him and went back forlornly along the New Guinea coast. After him no one came that way, or attempted the Drooge Bocht at all, until James Cook, ordered to find the "Southland," if there was such a place on the globe, insisted on forcing his way into high latitudes south of the trade-wind belt, and so evaded the hitherto impassable barrier.

Before we leave Carstensz altogether, we may as well note the results of his scrupulous exactitude. His pilot, Arend Martensz de Leeuw, put together a chart showing the route of the *Pera* and the shore-line it had made sure of. On this chart (which is in the Dutch archives at the Hague) there is a gap over three degrees wide between the ascertained shores of New Guinea and the ascertained shores of the new country. A belt of shallows—the Drooge Bocht—lies along the New Guinea coast; another belt runs north and south just west of the gap, with open sea marked at either end of it; off the mouth of the Jardine rises the mountainous Prince of Wales Island. No map could be more outspoken. It proclaims a passage, or at least says "As far as we know, there are three possible passages eastwards." On one man the lesson was not lost. Anthony van Diemen, Governor-General of the Dutch Indies in the 1640's, had no time to waste on Australia— the reports of many navigators assured him that it was a useless country—but he had great visions of trade with the South Sea Islands and perhaps with South America. In 1642 he sent off Abel Tasman to find out whether there was a way round New Holland into the Pacific; Tasman found it, running past the southern end of Tasmania and across to New Zealand, but reported that the route was beset with storms. In 1644, therefore, he was sent off again to follow up the indications given by Carstensz, and look for a passage eastwards either by the Drooge Bocht or by the

Gulf of Carpentaria. Van Diemen was especially eager about the Drooge Bocht route; his orders were that Tasman should cautiously cross the Bocht, anchor on the south side, and reconnoitre the land, sending the sloop attached to his expedition into the great bay to ascertain whether anywhere in it there was a passage to the South Seas. No orders could have been wiser. Where a ship could not crawl eastwards against the trades, a smaller vessel might hope to slip along under the lee of the high land until an opening appeared. What Tasman did we know not, but he certainly did not obey orders. The only records of his voyage are a chart showing solid land from the north to the south of the Bocht, a marked track on it showing that he did not make any attempt to enter the bight, a note on it to the effect that New Guinea and the South Land "form all one continent together," and a note on a copy of the chart, now in the British Museum, "This large land of New Guinea was first discovered to join ye South Land by ye Yot Lemmen," one of Tasman's vessels. ("First" is of course the significant word.) The probability is that Tasman, who was horribly afraid of landing anywhere where he might meet warlike savages (the mere trace of some scared him from Tasmania), dreaded a stay of several days on a coast where both the *Duyfken* and the *Pera* had encountered determined hostility, and simply ignored Van Diemen's instructions and saved himself trouble by drawing lines on the map.

Van Diemen at any rate was not hoodwinked. He was anxious for another attempt and outspokenly contemptuous of Tasman's botching:

> What there is in the South Land, whether above or underneath the earth, continues unknown, since the men have done nothing beyond sailing along the coast; he who makes it his business to find out what the land produces must walk over it.

His masters at The Hague, however, were not enthusiastic, and he died in 1645, and the matter was shelved. But Tasman's assertion that he had closed the gap was not widely accepted. Charts constructed with the help of his discoveries of 1644, themselves dating between 1647 and 1663, still show the Drooge Bocht as Carstensz had left it, and as late as 1685 one big Dutch official—Georg Rumpf, Governor of Amboyna—admitted his doubts. He writes of "the Drooge Bocht, where Nova Guinea is thought to be cut off from the rest of the South-land by a passage opening into the great South Sea, though shallows prevented our men from traversing it, so that it remains uncertain whether this strait runs right through."

In 1756 one last Dutch attempt was made to solve the mystery. Jean Etienne Gonzal and Lodewijk van Asschens sailed into the gulf and repeated Carstensz's northward coasting voyage as far as the Speult River. Anchoring there on 29 April, they sent off a boat to take soundings. They waited for it, signalling nightly, until 12 May, but dared not follow it into the teeth of the winds, which were persistently south-east or east-south-east. On the 13th they abandoned hope and departed westwards. The trades had kept the secret.

JOHN BLAXLAND

JOHN and Gregory Blaxland were by many years the forerunners of a class of settler to which Australia owes a very great deal. One is apt unthinkingly to connect early Australian settlement with (*a*) convicts, (*b*) assisted immigrants, (*c*) gold-seekers; learning a little more, one recognises also the pioneering work—pastoral and agricultural—done by early military and civilian officials (John Macarthur, Samuel Marsden and their like). But the men who in the 1820's and 1830's found energy and ardour enough to effect their slow permeation of the New South Wales inland country with flocks and herds and the essentials of civilisation—the men who twenty and thirty years later occupied and found use for that huge Queensland "outback" with which the British Government embarrassingly dowered a struggling, pauper administration at Brisbane—the brave and often wise gentlemen whom Henry Kingsley knew and drew for us in *Geoffry Hamlyn*—these were of a different type from the rest; they were sons, usually younger sons, of old British land-holding stock, who inherited with their blood the gift of managing estates and breeding stock and improvising on their own properties all the minor mechanisms that might be useful there. Even their migrations were individual. The move to the new oversea country once planned, these young captains of agriculture chartered or bought a vessel, loaded it with all the machines and utensils they expected to need, embarked their families and their farm-hands, chosen from the near-by villages, and departed into distant oceans a practically self-sufficing community. The records of the founding of Western and of South Australia are full of such communities, and it is hard to over-estimate their value to the Australia of those days, which sadly lacked skilled management and organised labour.

For this type of settlement the Blaxlands were the pioneers. They were hardly among the best; they lacked initiative, they preferred to proceed slowly and to use customary methods; when one of them opened for the colony the hitherto close-barred gates of the rich inland plains, neither he nor his brother seized the opportunity to exploit them. But they were the first non-official settlers, the first to choose New South Wales purely as a centre of farming operations and a home for their families. Living through troublous times—politically—in a thrice-disturbed society, they kept clear of politics and public life as long as they could, and aired few grievances that were not personal and concerned with their private business. Not the most public-spirited of citizens, maybe; but for that very reason all the better fosterers of colonial industries.

John Blaxland, born at Fordwich near Canterbury in Kent on 4 January, 1769, was a scion of an old Kentish family that felt itself deeply rooted in the soil. It cherished a belief that its ancestors had owned the Isle of Thanet, until the Conqueror evicted them. Less legendary was the claim that an ancestor had gone crusading with Richard Cœur de Lion, and another had been captain of the guard under Queen Elizabeth. A hamlet just beyond Fordwich preserved their name, and they owned at one time or another estates at Luddenham and Newington along the London-Canterbury road. Farming was in the Blaxland blood, and John, whose actual descent was from a branch that had migrated to Holborn, found himself more truly at home when in 1792 he left the army (in which he had reached the rank of captain in the Duke of York's cavalry) to inherit the family estates at Newington. But the family tradition was not of thrift; like his forefathers, John found it difficult to make income keep pace with expenditure; and in 1804, at the suggestion of Sir Joseph Banks,[1] he made up his mind to a great adventure. There were other Blaxlands to keep up the family name in the old county; moreover, the family's reputation for hospitality and lavish expenditure overburdened him, and a quieter life in a new country might straighten up his affairs. So he and his brother Gregory (about two years his junior) would transfer themselves, like patriarchs of old, to the far-off pastures of New Holland. As a farmer John was excellent; he planned his migration carefully, and bargained with the British Government soberly and providently. His demands (they were nominally Gregory's, but John inspired them) deserve study:

As we are likely to settle our families there for ever, to make demands contrary to the future interest of the colony would be improper, as the settlement is in its infancy. What encouragement we may receive in regard to grants of land may become a precedent in some measure to regulate the grants of future adventurers. Convinced nothing is more prejudicial to the interest of a rising colony than large tracts of land held by individuals, unoccupied, we make the following requests . . .

whereupon he asked for a primary grant of 6000 acres; after clearing, cropping, or using to the full for pasture at least 500 acres of this grant, a supplementary grant equal to the land utilised; in addition, 200 acres for every free servant brought out. As for stock, he proposed to buy 135 cattle and 206 sheep from Government stock, and 10 merinos from King George's famous flock; and he further asked for

[1] Banks was always on the look out for men with farming experience who might be persuaded to migrate to New Holland, and had a high opinion of John Blaxland both as a man and as an agriculturist.

the use of 30 convicts, to be fed for eighteen months at Government expense, and a free passage from England to Sydney. Gregory was to have the same. Needless to say, not even Banks's recommendation could procure him such terms. What was promised seems generous enough, daring though the migration must have appeared to men of those times, and worthy of exceptional rewards:

Provided John Blaxland engages a capital of £6000 in the colony of New South Wales, he is to be granted free passage for his family (self, wife, 4 or 5 children, 2 or 3 servants), 8000 acres of land, and 80 convicts who will be fed for 18 months at Government expense. If he cannot put down £6000, the grant and the labour will be reduced proportionately to the capital he does provide. Gregory the same.

Gregory—who could put down only £3000—was the first to go; naïvely enough, he wrote "I shall prefer going out in the ship with the female convicts." Among the stores for which he secured free transport were twelve merino sheep, four bulls, a swarm of bees, twelve trunks of clothing, seeds, ammunition, plants, glass, tools, a plough, wine, beer, cider, spirits, and "four cases for things forgot." After a thirty-two-weeks' voyage he reached Sydney on 11 April, 1806, and almost at once fell foul of Governor King, for whom the settlement was still a species of gaol, not to be lightly intruded on by strangers concerned only with their own livelihood. Still, King might have come to terms with the aliens; he was a hard-working, puzzle-headed, sincere old gentleman, anxious to straighten out the extremely tangled skein of the settlement's affairs, and ready—slowly—to appreciate and utilise other men's endeavours, however bizarre they might seem to him, so long as their goal lay in the same direction as his own. Had he remained in office long enough to discover that the Blaxlands were cheapening meat

John Blaxland

and dairy produce and breaking down the military officers' stranglehold on New South Wales commerce, he and they might have got on very well together. But in August 1806, before John Blaxland had reached the colony, King gave place to Bligh; and Bligh's theory of governing was that he had a mission to put right everything that King's deplorable weakness had allowed to go wrong, that everyone who asked for anything was probably trying to cheat the Government, and that nothing but stern refusals and drastic discipline could bring the unruly community back to a fit sense of its own disgraceful unworthiness. He much resembled the type of schoolmistress—rarer now than twenty years ago, thank Heaven!—who said to her assistants, "Find out for me what the girls want to do and I'll tell them they mustn't." So Gregory Blaxland—who, had Bligh but been able to discern it, would have proved quite a useful ally—found himself blocked at every turn when he tried to get the land and the labour that had been promised, and in the end found it best to lie low and await the arrival of his stronger and abler brother.

John had devised for himself a new method of migration. Chartering a whaler from the firm of Hullett Brothers (he ranked as part-owner of her), he loaded her up with his own belongings—including a wife, four children, a governess, two maids, a bailiff, a carpenter, and a boy-of-all-work—and used space still vacant to take out merchandise of sorts; he saw himself as a merchant (that was his Holborn training) as well as a farmer, with the Hulletts as his London agents. In the *Brothers* he reached Port Jackson on 4 April, 1807, provided with letters ordering Bligh to give him further concessions in lieu of the free passage he had been promised but had not availed himself of. If there was one thing Bligh particularly hated, it was an order from London to grant immigrants concessions. When he found himself bound to give Blaxland cattle from the Government herds, to be paid for by instalments of "produce," he obstinately insisted that "produce" meant "kind" (i.e. cattle), and that for the sixty cows Blaxland received at once he must hand back twenty young cows every second year. John might protest, and explain that the original intention had been that payment should be made in grain; Bligh was immovable. John had to accept the terms—and found himself forced to concentrate on cattle-breeding. Thorough in everything that had to do with farming, he took up 1200 acres of swamp below Parramatta (the only land Bligh would give him), embanked it against floods, constructed salt-pans along the edge of the tidal waters, started a dairy in Sydney with the milk of twenty-nine cows and sold there meat and vegetables as well as dairy produce; steadily undercutting the exorbitant prices previously charged by the pseudo-military New South Wales Corps farmers, he lowered the price of meat from 2s. 6d. to 1s. per lb., gave the settlement fresh butter and green vegetables such as it had never yet enjoyed, and improved the quality of the local salt until salted meat became an almost luxurious diet. His reward was that at the end of October Bligh devoted to his affairs a short dispatch in which the hope was expressed that "he will turn his mind to agricultural pursuits as well as the grazing of cattle," and in a longer, more querulous dispatch of the same date worked himself up to a denunciation of commercial economics that should really have been addressed to his other enemies, Macarthur and the Corps officers:

The Blaxlands, who lately came out, become so speculative as to care for nothing but making money; they endeavour to monopolise under a principle of buying as cheap as they can and selling dear.

Considering what John had achieved in the butchering trade, this was ungracious, but Bligh in anger hit the first man he thought of. One can understand, too, his point of view, if one pictures the plight of a battle-cruiser's captain, bound on an important mission, and forced at the same time to carry representatives of a private firm of victuallers anxious to push their trade both with the ship's provedore and at every port the ship enters.

One understands also why, when in January 1808 the New South Wales Corps mutinied and deposed Bligh, the Blaxlands were among the approvers of its action. They got no good of it, unfortunately; Macarthur, who for some months was the actual ruler of the colony, was John's personal enemy, and Colonel Johnston, the nominal ruler, grew irritated almost beyond endurance when John worried him to make the concessions that Bligh had refused. At last John decided to leave Gregory in charge and go himself to London to seek redress. He sailed in the *Rose* on 15 September, 1808, via Cape Town. But Bligh had heard of his going, and managed to get a letter sent by the same vessel to Lord Caledon (then Governor at the Cape) charging Blaxland with all the crimes of all the mutineers; John was taken off the vessel in Table Bay, clapped into a filthy Dutch prison—where he caught jail fever—and after a month shipped to England in H.M.S. *Powerful* and dragged in custody across his own home county to London. There he was set free, only to be re-arrested at Macarthur's instance for non-payment of a draft which Gregory, apparently, had forgotten to honour.

For three years he cooled his heels in England (being needed as a witness in the trial of Colonel Johnston for the Bligh mutiny), but eventually persuaded the authorities that he had been badly treated, and went back to New South

Wales with a letter to Macquarie ordering that the original agreement should at last be carried out in full. If he had arrived when Macquarie was new to his work, things might yet have gone smoothly. Gregory, however, after establishing amicable relations with the new Governor and even taking him on explorations along the Nepean River, had by John's arrival fallen out of favour. Macquarie, in all other ways as different from Bligh as a lion from a lynx, was as insistent as his predecessor on the necessity of team work and on the development of the settlement through agriculture. Simeon Lord, really a more commercially-minded man than either of the Blaxlands, won Macquarie's favour partly, of course, because he was a show-emancipist, but mainly because he was imaginative and enterprising along many branches of industry and manufacture that would employ a large number of colonists. Gregory had found favour first as a partner of Lord's; when it became apparent that he was not interested in the manufacturing side of his partner's enterprises, he was dismissed as lacking public spirit. And so John, returning to Sydney full of hope and determination to make his cattle-breeding as important to the colony as Macarthur's and Marsden's sheep-breeding, found himself faced by an angry Governor with this prejudice:

These two Gentlemen Settlers . . . coming hither, as they did, in the professed character of *Agriculturalists*, it would have been most naturally expected that they should have applied their personal and great acquired means of husbandry to the cultivation of Grain on a proportionately enlarged Scale. . . . Instead of contributing thus to the general welfare of the country, and setting a good example of an improved stile of farming and agriculture, they have turned their whole attention to the lazy object of rearing of cattle, and have been thus enabled to put into the Government Stores a quantity of fresh meat to the enormous amount of 88,936 lbs. within the space of two years and nine months. ... Within the same period they have not put into the Stores one single bushel of Grain of any kind whatever.

The encouragement of this description of persons called *Gentlemen Settlers* by extraordinary concessions in their favor has not heretofore contributed to the advancement of Agriculture in this Colony ... the Individuals thus benefitted, so far from showing a disposition to be grateful, are the most discontented unreasonable and troublesome persons in the whole country.— Macquarie to Lord Liverpool, 17 November, 1812.

The irate Governor had at least this excuse, that in 1812 the collapse of agriculture after a long drought had forced him to import wheat from India, and he felt vaguely that this need not have happened had the Blaxlands cropped their land instead of pasturing cattle on it. John's answer, however, was simple and sufficient—he had as yet been granted no land fit for crops. But Macquarie, excellent administrator as he was, was no farmer. His limited experience of cattle —which were not carefully tended in the Highlands—led him to believe that all a breeder did was to turn them out to pasture and leave the rest to Nature. The value of careful sheep-breeding he could understand, for improvements in wool-quality were unmistakable; careful cropping was just as unmistakably valuable, since it increased the yield of grain. But he could not grasp in the same way the value of cattle-breeding—though he might with a little thought have seen that the man who reduced the price of meat from 2s. 6d. in 1807 to 1s. in 1809, 9d. in 1811, and 7d. in 1813, deserved praise, not ill-tempered criticism. Blaxland's work for the colony was less spectacular than Macarthur's creation of the Australian merino sheep, and—because wool was exportable, whereas beef and milk were mainly articles of home consumption—less visibly important to the prosperity of the colony, but of great value nevertheless. If in 1810 the colony's horned cattle numbered about 10,000, in 1820 54,000, and in 1840 nearly 400,000, it was to the Blaxlands' care and example that the increase was largely due.

This has been the story not so much of John Blaxland's doings as of his sufferings, of the obstacles he had to surmount and the mistreatments he had to undergo. Obviously the story of a breeder's life is of little general interest, but one may appreciate his achievement by a narration of his chief discouragements. After a long tussle with Macquarie over the exact meaning of his original agreement and the evidence of his expenditure in New South Wales (in which Macquarie showed himself at his most meticulous and pernickety), John settled down to the serious work of his life. He took no advantage of the discoveries beyond the Blue Mountains which his brother had initiated, although in 1816 and afterwards stock-holders were allowed to send their herds across the range and graze them on the western plains. The Blaxlands looked northwards for preference to the Hunter valley, where their cattle could be travelled direct to the port of Newcastle through good pastures all the way, instead of being driven tediously across rough mountain roads, steep and grassless for fifty miles at least. Until the Hunter district was opened John possessed his soul impatiently at Luddenham near the Nepean, with his enemy John Macarthur just south of him at Camden and a number of smaller holders—mostly fellow-magistrates and friends—limiting his access to the river and the grazing-grounds beyond; he had more trouble with Macquarie over these lands also, since the Governor made up his mind that private owners must stay east of the river, and peremptorily ordered them to collect and withdraw their stock at once from the Crown lands beyond it. (It must be noted, though, that neither of the Blaxlands tried to intrigue against Macquarie, as did others of their equally aggrieved acquaintance; "discontented"—once "lazy discontented drones"—was his worst word for the brothers, but the others were repeatedly denounced in secret reports to Earl Bathurst as slanderers and intriguers.)

When in the early 1820's, under Governor Brisbane, the rich lands of the Hunter valley were thrown open to moneyed settlers, John Blaxland was happy again. By this time, however, cattle-breeding was ingrained in him; he left to younger men the exploitation of the river-flats and agricultural plains, and took up 8000 acres in the foothill country near Broke on the Wollombi, where his stock could camp on dry ground. Gregory for his part in 1825 made an attempt to establish salt-pans at Newcastle, so that the Blaxland cattle could be slaughtered and salted down close to their feeding-grounds. This enterprise failed, no one quite knows why; but Gregory was not a good business man, and there was a good deal of friction between the brothers. So, between Luddenham and Broke, John spent another twenty years of prosperous management. His children went farther afield, occupying stations beyond the settled areas both in New England and along the Murray, under the humorous system whereby stock-owners were forbidden to stray over the official border-line of the "settled districts," denounced as "trespassers" when they did stray, and then granted cheap licences to trespass (one of the sons was alleged in 1844 to occupy 610,000 acres of Murray lands on these conditions). But the patriarch was content to keep up his hospitable mansion at Newington in New South Wales as generously and showily as he might, with better luck in his early years, have played the "fine old English gentleman" at Newington in Kent. One thing only disturbed his peace—besides the chronic lack of funds for his squirearchy. He had acquired a habit of discontent with the Government. As late as 1827 Governor Darling was investigating all over again his complaints about Bligh's refusal to honour any promises and Macquarie's grudging fulfilment of some of them; on the whole, Darling thought, the old man had been badly treated, but his claims for compensation were too exorbitant to be admitted. To soothe him down, probably, he was nominated a member of the Legislative Council, in which he sat from January 1829 to January 1843, but distinguished himself mainly by registering annual protests against expenditure on immigrants and on New Zealand. In the first "representative" Council of 1843 he sat for a few months as a nominated member, but resigned in September 1844, and died peaceably at Newington on 5 August, 1845.

Apart from their work as breeders and meat-sellers the Blaxlands, in such a sketch as this, must inevitably figure as short-tempered and rather selfish citizens. They were at loggerheads with Bligh, with Macarthur, with Macquarie, with Brisbane—who made John a magistrate and cancelled the appointment within a year—occasionally with Darling (although Gregory's son married Darling's niece). This impression, if retained, would be very unjust to them. Towards the end of his life, no doubt, John became almost a professional grumbler, though this did not prevent the various Governors from renominating him steadily to the Council. But consider his early colonial experiences before hasty judgment is passed on him. In England he was valued both as an experienced farmer and as a member of a county family. Joseph Banks, a man of high standing and notable scientific attainments, when implored again and again to procure for New South Wales colonists with capital and practical farming experience, begged him to migrate and begged the Sydney authorities to treat him with generosity

John Blaxland

and respect. He left England a minor magnate, about to confer on a raw community the gifts of breeding and experience. He found himself in Sydney regarded by the Governor as a horse-leech, by the petty military bureaucracy as an interloper; anxious only to do the work he had been selected for, he was refused the land, limited as regarded labour, dragged unwillingly into local political squabbles of which he knew little and cared less, snubbed when he suggested the fulfilment of promises made to him by the authorities in England. Bligh and Macarthur between them made his return to England a purgatory; when he reached Sydney again, he was confronted with the solemn and not very intelligent disapproval of Macquarie. There was a good deal in all this to sour any man's temper.

That is the worst of being a pioneer. He reached Port Jackson twenty years too soon. Had he and his been younger —had they come to New South Wales with the inrush of young adventurers that followed the granting of a constitution and the downfall of autocracy—they would have been leaders of the squatter fraternity. As it was, John Blaxland was merely an early experimenter on whom reluctant Governors tried out their inexperience. That he came through the tests, fair and unfair, is the best evidence of his single-mindedness, his integrity, his concentration on the work set before him. The modern Australian, versatile, impatient, apt to alter his methods and his goals as readily as his pleasures and his hobbies, might do worse than study and occasionally imitate the Blaxland character.

GREGORY BLAXLAND

THE younger brother, Gregory Blaxland, who had been sent in advance by John in 1806, settled at South Creek near Penrith and occupied himself for years with his own farm and the management of John's affairs while he was away in England. Less energetic than his brother—though in the twenties he too contributed a good deal to the expansion of New South Wales agriculture—Gregory by a single exploit earned for himself and for the family name renown that would never have come their way through John's more persistent and enlightened farming experiments. This exploit was so epoch-making (one cannot apologise for using a familiar adjective when it is literally true) that it needs detailed consideration.

As a centre from which a colony may be developed Sydney is thoroughly unsuitable. Its choice was the act of seamen incited thereto by two accidents—Cook's landing in Botany Bay and his (or Banks's) erroneous belief that the reed-beds of George's River were excellent cattle-pastures. Had Cook sighted the Australian coast half a day earlier or later, he might have landed farther down the coast or farther north, but would have passed the heads of Botany Bay in the night. And had not one of his party waxed eloquent in London about the spreading grasslands and the "deep black soil . . . capable of producing any kind of grain," Phillip would not have found himself in January 1788 forced to make some sort of a settlement somewhere in the neighbourhood, without too much research, in order to set ashore without delay the 1482 persons who had for eight months been crowded aboard eleven small vessels of a total burthen of less than 4000 tons. Sydney once selected, its advantages as a harbour endeared it to the four naval governors who preceded Macquarie, and its huge disadvantages as a centre for growing settlement did not disturb them. After all, they were mainly gaolers of a special quality, intent on preserving discipline and therefore on hampering agricultural expansion, which must inevitably remove their prisoners from the strict control possible only in a compact community.

The disadvantages just hinted at were involved in the physical surroundings of the Sydney district. Five miles north, forty miles west and south-west, and less than ten miles to southward, the more or less fertile soil of the Port Jackson hinterland merged into barren, rock-strewn, uncultivable hills through which it seemed impossible to find a way. To this day there is no direct road from Sydney north to Newcastle, and only a mediocre road from Sydney towards the valley of the Hunter. Southwards for fifty miles beyond George's River there stretches a barren plateau of sandstone that makes an excellent catchment area for the Sydney water-supply, but has no other possible value and is almost undisturbed by the most primitive traffic. Westwards the land undulates, cultivable but not really fertile, towards the great stream of the Hawkesbury, where the rich soil is often flooded and the unfloodable soil never rich. And from the farther bank of the Hawkesbury rises steeply, in most parts still impassably, the ridged edge of the Blue Mountain plateau. For a hundred and fifty miles along it, from the Goulburn River in the north to the Upper Wollondilly, only three practicable tracks traverse it—one by a good road and a railway, one by a road that has been made possible for wheeled traffic only during this century, one still a "stock-route" allowing the passage of stock, mounted men, and pedestrians.

It was this enormous barrier that stifled the young colony's expansion as soon as the comparatively fertile patches of eastern soil were occupied by growers of wheat and maize. When enterprising colonists, following the lead of John Macarthur, began to demand large pasture-lands for their sheep, attempts to break through the barrier became importunate. In 1789-90 exploring parties had climbed the first ridge only to find behind it rougher ridges interspersed with precipitous-sided gorges. In 1793 a boat-party worked its way for ten miles up one of these gorges, that of the Grose, and after five difficult portages retreated to the coast. In 1794 two or three adventurous seamen crossed, according to their own account, "eighteen or nineteen ridges of high rocks" without finding a way out of the mountains. In 1796 George Bass—the discoverer of the strait named after him—struggled for fifteen days up and across the high land, taking infinite trouble to lower himself into the deep valleys as soon as he had attained a height; by that time thoroughly sick of his task, he sighted another range forty miles to westward, and decided to come back. In 1798 a more southward route was attacked by an ex-convict with the Governor's approval; had he been well provisioned and ready for a two-months' march, Wilson might have rounded the ridge at the Goulburn end—as it was, he returned with reports too exciting to be believed, and as a matter of fact founded on miscalculations. In 1802, however, Francis Barrallier started along Wilson's track with more elaborate preparations, penetrated to the heart of the mountains as directly westerly as was possible, and by sheer ill-luck, when he was less than ten miles from the summit of the range, turned north into a deep gorge that ended in precipitous cliffs. The most persevering of his tribe, George Caley (one of Joseph Banks's botanists), made several ineffective dashes against the barrier, the last in 1806; and then the ridge had rest for six years.

Gregory Blaxland, living on South Creek within a few miles of the ridge, and interested in any possibilities of expansion that would give him and his brother more room for their herds, indulged occasionally in a mild exploration and more frequently in a bout of hard thinking. While his brother was in England he managed to keep on good terms with Macquarie, whose wife found him "a pleasant and facetious companion." During those friendly days he once took the Governor some miles up a torrential stream that issued from the mountains near by, and then unfolded to the intrigued guest a scheme for crossing those hitherto impenetrable ridges by avoiding the valleys along which previous explorers had tried to make their way and seeking persistently the highest available crests. Strangely enough, about the same time another settler, William Lawson of Prospect, was thinking along the same lines. He was an old officer of the New South Wales Corps, skilled in the rough survey-work of those days, and had discussed the problem frequently with George Caley; and his conclusion was that the summit-levels would afford the easiest pathway because "the timber and scrubby underwood would there be thinnest, and a long continuous flat or table land[1] would offer much smaller impediments." Priority cannot safely be given to either proponent. Blaxland afterwards claimed to have originated the method of traverse and suggested it to Macquarie, with whose approval he invited Lawson and

[1] This remark shows that earlier explorers had somehow discerned the true quality of the Blue Mountains ridge as the remains of a table-land rather than a sierra or normal mountain range.

Wentworth to accompany him; Lawson never himself made any claim, but friends some years later claimed for him (and were not contradicted) that he had devised the method, and had taken along Wentworth as an agreeable companion and Blaxland as a persevering assistant. The chances are that Macquarie, who was at the moment friendly with both men, tactfully arranged the party himself.

On 11 May, 1813, the three explorers, accompanied by four convicts, crossed the Nepean near Penrith and next day started up the ridge. Momentous as the journey was to prove, it had nothing really exciting about it, no such romantic setting as was to hand for the early penetrators of Pyrenean or Alpine passes. The actual clambering necessary could be matched and surpassed any day by a dozen routes among the hills of Cumberland. Down in the valleys there was danger and difficulty enough, for most of them were hopelessly encumbered with enormous boulders and blocked at the end with remarkable precipices; but, once it was determined to avoid the valleys and stay above the precipices, the task of crossing was merely tiresome. The chief obstacle was the stubbornness of the undergrowth, which often made it necessary to leave the horses in camp for a day or two while a track was being hewn through the scrub. Blaxland's journal, a straightforward and quite uninspired account of the proceedings from day to day, lays its chief stress on the "scrubby undergrowth" and the "thick brushwood" through which on their fourth day out they cut a five-mile path and on the fifth only a two-mile. After noon on the third day they found no signs of human habitation during ten days' travel, the barrier having been as impenetrable to blackfellows as to Europeans. Indeed, loneliness marked the whole ridge; "the track of scarcely any animal was to be seen, and very few birds"; once they heard an emu calling, once the howling of native dogs, and their own dogs killed three kangaroos. The drudgery, and the loneliness, and the mystery proved their greatest dangers, for the convicts' nerves were affected. When on the first Sunday out the expedition had a rest, Blaxland records that he

> had reason to regret this suspension of their proceedings, as it gave the men leisure to ruminate on their danger; and it was for some time doubtful whether on the next day they could be persuaded to venture farther.

Persuaded, however, they were, and the following Sunday was *not* made a day of rest.

Keeping to the top of the ridge was no straightforward business; it ran "sometimes in a north-north-west direction, sometimes south-east, or due south, but generally south-west or south-south-west." Also there was no water on the crest, and when six days out they had to fetch it up a precipice about 600 feet high, getting scarcely enough for the men and none for the horses. Next day they encountered the only patch of genuine rock-climbing in the whole journey:

> The ridge, which was not more than fifteen or twenty yards over, with deep precipices on each side, was rendered almost impassible (*sic*) by a perpendicular mass of rock, nearly thirty feet high, extending across the whole breadth, with the exception of a small broken track in the centre.

However, it needed only the removal of a few large stones to get the horses through; and from that day onwards they were travelling along a broader plateau with swamp grass for the horses and plenty of water for everyone. On the 22nd they reached what seemed to be the summit of the range, a stony common of about 2000 acres, lightly grassed, with a splendid view but no possible way of descent; its cliff-boundary, sandstone precipices averaging 400 feet in height, "divided the interior from the coast as with a stone wall," beyond which they saw the whole Sydney area and a huge region of barren and contorted country towards the south and west. Much disappointed, they turned north along the plateau, Sunday though it was; weary convicts could not be given time for more rumination in such circumstances.

But the end of their troubles was at hand. On Monday they heard natives near by, on Tuesday they saw tracks of a wombat, on Wednesday there were native camp-fires in the valleys below. They had by now passed the real summit of the ridge, and were skirting the precipices of the great Kanimbla valley, forty miles wide, that train-travellers to-day watch from their carriage windows after a three-hour journey from Sydney; Blaxland had reached the same point after more than a fortnight's journey from Penrith, only forty miles away. On the 28th they found themselves on a jutting peninsula edged on one side with precipices, on the other with very steep grass slopes, down which the horses were led with the aid of a trench cut with hoes across its contours. To their surprise and delight "they discovered that what they had supposed to be sandy barren land below the mountain, was forest land, covered with good grass, and with timber of an inferior quality"; and on the 29th their way lay through open meadows covered with grass two to three feet high. That Sunday (the 30th) could safely be made a day of rest, though a thick frost discouraged loafing, and they hunted kangaroos for relaxation. And on the Monday they enjoyed themselves—they walked over six miles of excellent and well-watered pasture to a sugar-loaf hill, whence they

descried all around, forest or grass land, sufficient in extent, in their opinion, to support the stock of the Colony for the next thirty years.

From their point of view (as stock-breeders) their work was

done. On 1 June they turned back to the foot of the trenched hill (nowadays known as Mount York) and, rapidly retracing their steps along the marked track, on the night of the 3rd heard a confused noise arising from the eastern settlements below, which, after having been so long accustomed to the death-like stillness of the interior, had a very striking effect.

On the 5th, quaintly enough, they were almost hopelessly "bushed" on the eastern slope of the ridge within a few miles of Penrith, so perverse was the undergrowth in that district; on the morning of the 6th they forded the Nepean after breakfast, and scattered to their several homes.

And what happened then? For the men who had broken through that stubborn barrier one might expect some welcome —not processions and bands,. perhaps, which were beyond the resources of a small convict colony, but some kind of public recognition of their achievement. What did happen was . . . nothing at all. Blaxland went back to South Creek and Lawson to Prospect; Wentworth slipped away to the South Seas, sandalwood-trading; Macquarie noted the discoveries and pondered over them, but neither said nor did anything for five months. Then he sent for George William Evans, at the time assistant-surveyor in Tasmania, and dispatched him on 19 November to find out what there really was beyond the mountains. When in January 1814 Evans returned with news of great rivers and open fertile plains not 150 miles away, Macquarie burst into eulogy. Everything Evans had done was excellent and invaluable, worthy of great reward from the British Government; Blaxland and his companions were casually mentioned in a "general order" in February 1814, but their work was not announced to the authorities in London till June 1815, when Macquarie himself had crossed the ranges and founded Bathurst.

This neglect to acknowledge merit has puzzled everyone who has considered it, from Gregory himself onwards, and has somewhat damaged in historians' eyes Macquarie's reputation for fair dealing. Some explain it as a manifestation of the Governor's dislike for the Blaxland family—but Macquarie had no dislike for Lawson, and was very friendly with the Wentworths. The most probable explanation is that, until he actually saw the difficulties they had surmounted, he was not especially impressed with their exploit. They were, after all, not deeply impressed with it themselves at the time. They had solved an important problem and carried through a worrying and wearisome job, and there was an end of it. Only ten years later did Gregory think it worth while to print his journal, and in the same year Wentworth (who in 1820 had not thought it worth while even to mention the exploit in which he had shared) broke out into a grandiose eulogy, for Cambridge consumption, of the "mighty ridge" and the "beauteous landscape" seen from Mount York. As for Macquarie, when in 1815 he crossed the ranges by his newly made road, and viewed the tangles they had penetrated and the precipices they had confronted, his acknowledgment (in his dispatch to the Colonial Office) was full and hearty. But in 1813 all he knew was that they had gone a long way—"not without much labour, perseverance and fatigue," as George Evans rightly said—to discover only some good cattle-pastures amid distant hills very difficult of access. Sheep-breeders and cattle-men might think that good news; but Macquarie's vision of his spreading domain was not inspired solely by thoughts of cattle and sheep. His most serious complaint about John Blaxland, as we have seen, was that he preferred cattle to wheat; why should he wax enthusiastic because the younger Blaxland had found a little more cattle-country? "Labour and fatigue," yes; but Macquarie was a soldier, accustomed to a career in which endless labour and fatigue was part of the day's work, and the capture of a minor outpost was not necessarily made the subject of a General Order.

But . . . when George Evans brought back next year the news of Bathurst Plains—

The soil is exceedingly rich and produces the finest grass intermixed with variety of herbs; the hills have the look of a park and Grounds laid out; I am at a loss for language to describe the country. . . .
A finer Country than I can describe, not being able for want of language to dwell on the subject, or explain its real and good appearance with Pen and Ink, but assure you there is no deception in it—

and told how day after day he had travelled through well-watered, sparsely timbered plains abounding with life, Macquarie felt that there indeed was the promise of wide territories and rich farm-lands on which a nation might be nurtured. This land was worth reaching at once. In July he set William Cox (a near neighbour of the Blaxlands and already a noted road-builder) to make a carriage road along the track; by the end of the next January the road was completed into the plains, and in April 1815 Macquarie traversed it in nine days and signified his approval in the usual way—Adam's. The town he founded was named after the Secretary for the Colonies, Earl Bathurst; the river it stood on after himself; the pass down Mount York (grade one in four, impassable for loaded vehicles on the up journey) and a neighbouring stream took their names from Cox; the three pioneers had to be content with a hearty eulogy, 1000 acres of land for each (in the new western country, if they chose[1]), and their names attached—by Evans, as a matter of fact—to three hills in the bush near the farthest point they had attained. Evans himself, who had gone back to Tasmania, had nothing at all named after him.

It should be added that, whoever originated the method of crossing the Blue Mountains, Lawson was both the central figure and the most methodical of the explorers. All three kept diaries; Wentworth's is the spasmodic, excited, comparatively useless composition of a boy on his first big adventure; Blaxland's is a sober account, not very systematic (he frequently forgets to enter distances), but full of details of the surrounding scenery and the quality of the country traversed; Lawson's is a painstaking record, quarter-mile by quarter-mile, of the distances paced and the directions pursued, so exact that by plotting it on transparent paper and superposing it on a map of the district one can follow every step of the route and calculate how nearly Lawson's scale of paces corresponded to the actual mileage accomplished. Nor did Lawson abandon, as his companions did, the task of opening up the inland country. Macquarie made him commandant at Bathurst in 1819, and in the next three years he established communications behind the range through remarkably puzzling country into the Hunter valley.

Gregory was not of the true exploring breed; his pioneering was done otherwise. About 1819 he left South Creek and bought from William Cox Brush Farm on the Parramatta,

---

[1] Of the three only Lawson took up western land. Wentworth —or his father for him—chose eastern land, and Blaxland at first opted for a block on the Illawarra coast. In 1816 he sold his option to a friend, who altered the location to one not twenty miles from Sydney, where now is the capital's noble southern playground of Cronulla.

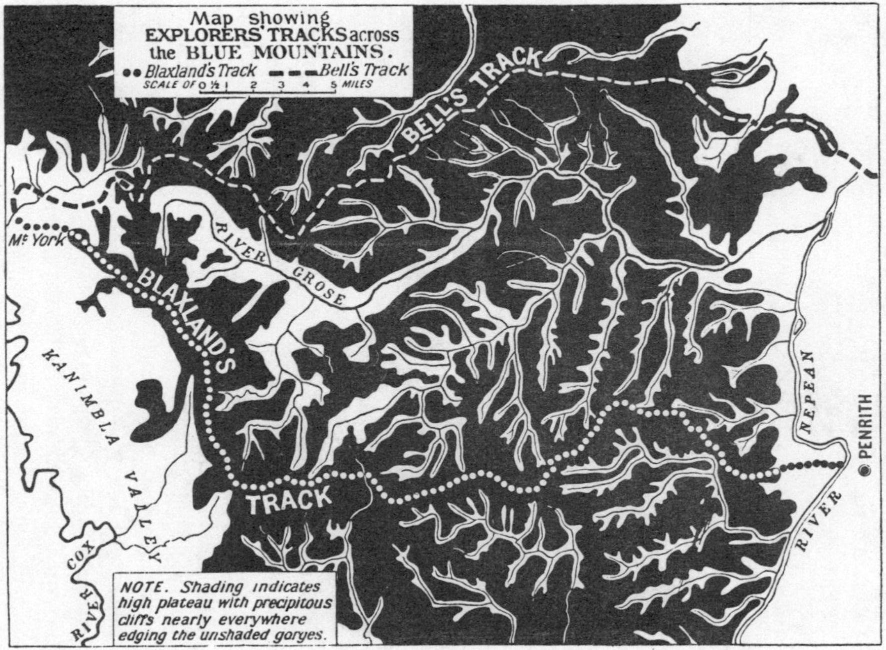
Map showing
EXPLORERS' TRACKS across
the BLUE MOUNTAINS.
Blaxland's Track
Bell's Track
SCALE OF 0 ½ 1 2 3 4 5 MILES
BELL'S TRACK
Mt York
RIVER GROSE
BLAXLAND'S TRACK
KANIMBLA VALLEY
RIVER COX
NEPEAN RIVER
PENRITH
NOTE. Shading indicates high plateau with precipitous cliffs nearly everywhere edging the unshaded gorges.

near John's headquarters at Newington. Here he experimented with various forms of agriculture, trying out several fodder-plants, introducing the useful buffalo-grass, and accustoming Sydney to the use of oaten hay when the native grasses were found unsuitable for mowing. Inspired by John, too, he started salt-pans on the lower Hunter, but after a two-year attempt to make them pay abandoned the enterprise. His real success in this line was made with vine-growing and wine-making. In 1819 he imported vine-stocks from the Cape of Good Hope; in 1823 he exported to London wine that gained him a silver medal from the Royal Society of Arts, and in 1828 secured its gold medal. At that time he was prominent enough as a citizen to be chosen by a big public meeting at Sydney to take to England a petition demanding trial by jury and some form of representative government. Thus, however, he fades out of history; we know where, during the next twenty-five years, he occasionally lived, and where at the end of them he died, but practically nothing more. Far less stable, far less useful on the whole than his elder brother, he lives in the memory of men and children who probably have never known he had a brother. For almost by sheer accident he was the first of that long line of adventurers—who count Sturt their most heroic and Augustus Gregory their most successful fellow—through whose indomitable courage and inexhaustible resourcefulness British Australia has been dowered with a continent for a home.

Note

Evidence of the interest taken in Australian affairs even as early as 1815, and of the lack of knowledge concerning them, is afforded by an audacious hoax played on the *Gentleman's*

Magazine regarding the passage of the Blue Mountains. In January 1815 that reputable and learned journal published the first part of an account of the crossing of the Blue Mountains "by an Officer of the 101st Reg." It is not easy to conceive why anyone should have taken so much—and at the same time so little—trouble over this hoax. The description of the range itself and of the methods employed to surmount it is as elaborate as it is inaccurate. The alleged mountains face towards Sydney for a hundred miles as a sheer cliff with a "regular perpendicular height of about three hundred feet"; they are climbed by contriving rough ladders up the gorge of the Cataract River, which empties itself into Shark's Bay. (The nearest English parallel to this would be an ascent of Skiddaw by penetrating a gorge through which the Tees empties itself into Pegwell Bay.) At the top of the gorge the explorers find bones of a mysterious animal with "the head and body of a bear, and tail similar to that of a crocodile, only smaller." The plateau beyond is covered with "stupendous columns of basalt, studded with a silvery copper ore." At this point the narrative breaks off, to be continued in our next; but—in June the editor gently intimated that he did not propose to continue it "till we can better authenticate the genuine history." Not till February 1817 was he able to fulfil his promise by reprinting Macquarie's official narrative of the true crossing, dated 10 June, 1815.

SIMEON LORD

AMONG those emancipist protégés for whom Macquarie sacrificed the harmonious administration of his colony, and the friendship of men nearer his own standard in culture and social graces, two stand out as fully worthy of the sacrifice. William Redfern was a good surgeon and a painstaking settler; Henry Fulton was an estimable parson and schoolmaster; Michael Robinson a poet laureate no worse than Britain in those days produced; James Meehan a hard-working surveyor and explorer. All four were worthy of encouragement, but scarcely outstanding enough among their fellows to justify a Governor in imperilling his power and influence for their sakes alone. A Governor's duty is to his subjects as a whole, and he may not lightly antagonise the most important of them merely to show favour—however well merited—to a few individuals.

Among his favourites, however, were two whose subsequent work for the good of the colony justified any help he chose to give them. It would be difficult to find two contemporaries of the same social standing more unlike each other than Simeon Lord and Francis Greenway, but each filled a niche in the social edifice Macquarie was erecting that—as far as one can judge—no other men in the colony could have filled, and each influenced the development of New South Wales (and therefore of Australia) along lines that have not yet been effaced.

Of Simeon Lord's youth we know very little; we do not even know for certain why he was transported. Davey, ex-administrator of Tasmania, in 1817 said he had been a pickpocket; but Davey was a disappointed man and Lord's enemy. Commissioner Bigge, who was no emancipist's friend and was doing his best to run Lord down, had to admit that the original offence had been "insignificant." All we know is that Lord reached Sydney in the convict-transport *Atlantic* on 20 August, 1791, and was assigned as servant to an officer of the New South Wales Corps. One way of serving your master in those days and circumstances was to manage a little business for him—very much as slaves in the days of Demosthenes were allowed to become merchants and bankers for their owners' profit—and Lord developed such usefulness in this direction that within a few years he was freed from servitude and allowed to go into business for himself. In 1800 we find him an active member of a syndicate which persuaded Governor Hunter to let it buy goods direct from trading vessels that might enter Port Jackson; as the officers of the Corps had hitherto arrogated this privilege to themselves, and had built up a dangerous monopoly thereby, Hunter was only too glad to find them some rivals. Sure now of a good income, Lord took a partner, Hugh Meehan (no relative of James), and the two purchased from the Crown a small prize—the *Anna Josepha*, a Spanish brig of 170 tons—and began to trade with other British settlements along the Australian coast. Things prospered with him exceedingly. In 1802 he added auctioneering to his other occupations, and soon afterwards, during the ephemeral Peace of Amiens, entered into contracts with Frenchmen from the Mauritius for a supply of spirits and with uncertain Americans to bring the goods across. In 1805 it was reckoned that he and his partners had over £12,000 sunk in whaling and sealing ventures. He fell foul of Governor Bligh, who gaoled him for a month and was severely reprimanded for so doing by the Colonial Office; he quarrelled with John Macarthur (which was easy but risky) and formed a partnership with the Blaxlands which grieved both Bligh and his successor Johnston; he made himself, in fact, thoroughly disliked by all the big men in the colony because they were thinking in terms of policies and partisanships while he was concerned only with trade and profits.

Why, then, need he be discussed at all here? and how did a man of his type attract the favourable notice of Macquarie, who objected to the Blaxlands on that very ground?

Because, astonishingly enough, he had imagination. He was always reaching out for new trade worlds to conquer. Auctioneering and whaling and trafficking in spirits and imported British merchandise would have given him wealth enough without much effort; others, free men at that, were satisfied with such unexciting pursuits. But Lord in his way was as much an adventurer as any great explorer. He liked riches, but he liked better the chase after them in unexploited fields. Just as for his spirits he went when he could to the Mauritius, so he ventured his money in pearl-fishing (more than fifty years before it became a recognised Australian industry) in 1808, and the Maori trade in 1809, and iron-mining in 1812, and sandalwood-trading in 1813. As we shall see, none of these ventures was profitable, but he was not discouraged; he became the first cloth-maker on a large scale, the first manufacturer of dyes and elaborate pottery, the first to back experiments with wattle-bark for tanning. It was this initiative in him that appealed to Macquarie, who reckoned it an excellent form of public spirit, and forgave many defects in manners and morals so long as a man had the civic virtues.

Consider first Lord's attempts to open a trade with New Zealand. Sealers and timber-getters had for some time paid regular visits to the New Zealand coast, and had established a disorderly settlement at the Bay of Islands almost due east of Sydney, often recruiting deck-hands among the local tribes and marrying Maori women. Lord's own sealers frequented the bay. But Lord saw clearly that nothing of permanent value was to be expected from such irregular colonisation, and looked about for some article of export on which a permanent trade might be based. He thought he had found it in the New Zealand flax-plant (*Phormium tenax*), whose fibre had been highly praised by Sir Joseph Banks and experimented with under King at Norfolk Island and in Sydney. Under his enemy Bligh he dared not make an obvious move in this direction; Bligh would have blocked him, and others might have borrowed the idea; but he began to establish a more definite connection with the Maori tribes by regularising the timber trade and studying the tribal tastes. (These tastes, in actual fact, ran chiefly to firearms and ammunition, for fighting was the Maori national sport, and a few muskets were invaluable in winning matches.) He began unluckily. In October 1809 he chartered the *Boyd* — a convict transport returning without such passengers to England—to carry home "2230 fine salted fur skins" (i.e. sealskins) and call at Whangaroa Harbour on the way to pick up a further cargo of spars. Among her crew was Tarra (or Mattarra), a chief of the Whangaroa tribe; he misbehaved during the voyage, and the master of the *Boyd* had him flogged.[1] A Maori chief's person is sacred, and his back more especially sacred than any other part of him except his head. Tarra's flogging amounted in Maori eyes to sacrilege. However, justice having been done, the

[1] It does not appear that the master knew he was flogging a chief; nor is it likely that he would have forborne to flog him had he known.

Boyd put in to Whangaroa; the tribe took two days to think things over, and then raided and looted the vessel, slaughtering all the Europeans aboard except a woman, a boy, and two small children who were rescued by a neighbouring chief[1] of higher standing.

Before the *Boyd* disaster was known in Sydney, Lord had found himself free of both his important enemies (Bligh and Johnston) and was planning his next move. His firm — since January 1810 styled Lord & Williams — joined Alexander Riley and Thomas Kent in forming a syndicate to import and manufacture *Phormium* fibre, and took in as interpreter and *liaison* official a remarkable emancipist named George Bruce, who had in 1806 married Te Pehi's youngest daughter and been adopted into the tribe, had been kidnapped with his wife by a visiting trader, and had just returned to Sydney after a fantastic adventure in which he had been fêted by the Indian Governor-General as "Heir Apparent to the Throne of New Zealand and Commander-in-Chief of the Maori armies." Kent was to be local manager in New Zealand, but it was thought that Bruce's connection with Te Pehi might be useful.

Macquarie had not been a month in office when Lord and his friends approached him with their scheme. They proposed to buy land near the Bay of Islands and in other *Phormium* districts, to establish flax-plantations, and to manufacture in New South Wales cordage and canvas for local

[1] This chief, Te Pehi, was an excellent old gentleman who had visited Sydney and become very friendly both with Governor King and with Samuel Marsden. His intervention in the *Boyd* affair was disastrous to himself. Known to have gone aboard the looted vessel, he was suspected by some whaling crews of instigating the massacre, and his village was burnt in revenge. Then the Whangaroa tribe, enraged with him for rescuing from them a part of their lawful prey, found him defenceless and killed him.

and naval use. Macquarie approved promptly, and agreed with them that a fourteen-year monopoly of the flax trade would not be unreasonable; this, however, he could not grant himself, but must refer it to London. Before an answer could be received news came of the *Boyd* massacre; Riley and Kent immediately backed out of their agreement, and Lord's chances of meeting the blow (he lost £12,000 worth of sealskins) were not bettered when Bruce claimed loudly that this was Te Pehi's revenge for the kidnapping of his dear son-in-law. That was the end of Bruce, but not of Lord; he merely hunted up another partner, found one (Andrew Thompson) who was a favourite of Macquarie's and had a good schooner of his own, and tried to improve on the *Boyd* venture with another returning transport, the *Experiment*. This vessel was to pick up at the Bay of Islands a cargo of dried flax ("as many tons as you can procure") and hand it over to the British authorities to be tested as to its value for ships' cordage. But the *Boyd* disaster had bitten in too deeply, the *Experiment's* master was panic-stricken, dared not search for cargo along the shores of the bay, and reported that he could procure only four pounds of flax. Lord's optimism failed him at last; he turned to iron-mining and sandalwood-trading, and the long-delayed refusal of the British Council of Trade to grant the monopoly he had asked for in 1810 did not disturb him in the least. In 1815, it is true, he and four others (among whom was W. H. Hovell the explorer) revived the New Zealand scheme in a slightly expanded form, proposing to create a company and invite the public to contribute part of the capital. But Macquarie, although he commended the proposal, on this occasion disapproved of the monopoly on which again Lord wished to base business, and the company was never formed.

Lord, in fact, was by this time well into his forties, and preferred to restrain his commercial adventurousness within the bounds of the colony. He still contemplated rope-making, but from English flax with the aid of Hindu experts; in 1815 he had three Bengalis in his employ. But new interests had already been aroused in him by the arrival, early in 1812, of one John Hutchison (or Hutchinson), transported for forgery. John was an amateur chemist of sorts, and had been the shining light of a scientific circle in York, where he had used the wood of the "Botany Bay Oak" (*Casuarina stricta*) to create dyes applicable to both wool and cotton. Consequently strong influence had been employed to secure for him transportation instead of hanging—the punishment proper to his offence—and the Society for the Encouragement of Arts, Manufactures and Commerce recommended him enthusiastically to Macquarie as a research worker who might "furnish particular Accounts of an infinite Variety of the natural products of New South Wales hitherto little known." Macquarie passed him on to Lord, who tried him out on various enterprises and found him a failure in all; "so very unsteady is he in all his Pursuits, that I can scarcely believe his Researches on any subject will be of the least importance to the World." Hutchison's notion apparently was that the colony should furnish him with a water-mill, a three-roomed laboratory, and complete sets of what he called "Chymerical Apparatus," including a number of not easily procurable reagents, should provide also skilled labour to run the mills, furnaces, etc., and should support him while he experimented in the void to see what would happen. Faced with masses of raw material and the scantiest means for handling it, his amateurishness became disconsolate and ineffective, and he sank into obscurity. He did prove the value of green wattle bark for tanning—but even so he invented an artificial distinction between the tanning "principle" in the bark and the astringent "principle"; "the Tanning Principle," he wrote, "is more Solueable than the Astringent." Lord set him to study the possibilities of making cloth, pottery and glass locally, but got nothing from him except a carding-machine and one for wire-drawing; but he claimed (it does not appear how truly) to have been successful also in the manufacture of soap and paint, and of white paper from a mixture of coloured rags and fig-tree bark.

It is not Hutchison that matters, but his effect on Lord. How much the carding-machine had to do with it we know not, but thenceforward Lord was primarily a cloth - manufacturer. He was probably the first man to make cloth directly from Australian-grown wool; he was certainly the most persistent and successful. Even Bigge, prejudiced against him for other reasons, waxed almost eloquent about the "industrious, intelligent manufacturer" who had "with great industry and success established manufactories of cloth and hats that have been very beneficial to the colony." Bigge's conclusion, however, is to be noted, for his spiritual descendants are still alive; Lord had done so well that he must be discouraged, or British trade might suffer.

As I do not conceive that it is consistent with the policy by which this country has always been guided, to encourage in any of her colonies, the establishment and growth of manufactures . . . I think that no encouragement should be given, in the shape of convict skill and labour, to such manufactures as interfere with either object, or that require a number of men to be confined to one spot. The only manufactures hitherto established are those of Mr. Lord, for coarse cloths, stockings, and blankets, and two for hats. From the specimens of these articles that I have brought with me from New South Wales, your Lordship will be enabled to form a judgment of the progress that has already been made in New South Wales in the manufacture of a principal article of export from the mother country, and of the expediency of discontinuing any encouragement to its further progress.—Bigge's *Report* No. 1, p. 158.

By 1824 Lord's mills near the shores of Botany Bay were among the "sights" of Sydney, and distinguished foreign tourists (e.g. the officers of Duperrey's expedition) were taken to have luncheon with him there and to admire the wide lagoon, the stately black swans, the shores bordered with flowering shrubs that in France would have adorned orangeries. There he made his last home, and there he died.

Another of the Hutchison-instigated enterprises he followed up for a good many years with less success. The use of the native "wattle" (*Acacia decurrens*) for tanning appealed to him, and when Hutchison dropped out he looked about him for someone to continue the experiments. After some years he discovered that an old (and a rather disappointing) associate, Thomas Kent, was working on the same problem in Tasmania. Kent had originally come to Australia in 1808 with a sheaf of valuable credentials and a plan for growing hemp mainly at the Government's expense. As no Governor would either import Asiatic labour for him or give him a seven-year monopoly of the hemp trade, Kent fell back on Lord and his New Zealand scheme, and (as we have seen) was scared out of that by the *Boyd* massacre. About this time Macquarie seems to have found out what manner of man he was, and Kent thought it wiser to settle in Tasmania; there, too, Macquarie's warnings followed him, and for the next six years he made a living by provisioning whalers, and amused himself with pin-pricking officials on any chance excuse. In 1818, however, we find him — either self-stimulated or prompted by Lord—engaged in attempts to procure tannin from wattle-bark and soda from the local seaweeds, both on a commercial scale. In 1819 Lord definitely commissioned him to make up both tannin and soda in quantity and proceed to England to take manufacturers' opinions on the products. Within a year he had sent off two tons of tannin extract, and was—he told Bigge—preparing for the visit to England, Lord having guaranteed that the experiments should be carried on during his absence. Unfortunately he was falling deeper and deeper into debt all the time; his departure for England was unduly hurried, and seems to have disgusted Lord finally with the backing of plausible adventurers; when next (in 1825) the tannin problem comes up, two new experimenters are associated with it, and Lord's name appears no more.

Remains for mention the side of his life—in reality the least important—which brought him into contact with Marsden and Molle and Bigge, and helped to embitter Macquarie's last years of rule. Macquarie when he first reached Sydney was much impressed with the sound common sense of Foveaux, who had inherited the administration from the anti-Bligh mutineers and had decided to occupy himself, until the home authorities should take action, with repairing the Sydney roads, reforming the local police, and vastly improving the discipline of the public service. That was a man after Macquarie's own heart, and any friend of his must be worth helping. Accordingly, when Foveaux commended Lord, also a man of common sense and public spirit, the new Governor thought he had lit upon exactly the right type of deserving emancipist to advance in proof of his own theories. In May 1810 Lord was made a magistrate, and became a frequent guest at Government House, where Mrs. Macquarie probably found his manners no worse than those of most of her free guests. There was a hint of coming trouble when Macquarie nominated him and Andrew Thompson (another emancipist) to sit on a road board with Samuel Marsden. Marsden disliked emancipists on principle, and had special reasons (so he said) for objecting to be associated publicly with two men of known immorality —he, a clergyman! One cannot test the truth of this allegation; but no man then living was more pious and more strict in the matter of morals than Macquarie himself, and it is extremely unlikely that he would have opened Government House doors to any notorious evil-liver. As it was, he took trouble to show his confidence in Lord—who, to do him justice, did not at any time put himself forward, and was accepted as a fellow-magistrate by other free men —and in 1818 appointed him one of the assessors of the Supreme Court, sitting with Judge Barron Field (who did not like it at all). We gather from the stories circulated about Lord in this connection that he was unobjectionable as a judge but undignified and illiterate; Field's charge that he was too much biased in favour of emancipists is not supported by definite instances, and at the worst merely signifies that Field himself was less gentle with them. However, when Bigge began to harry Macquarie about his predilection for ex-convicts, and stories of Lord's malapropisms found ready circulation—they were no worse than are told nowadays of sheriffs and justices in the Middle United States—Macquarie sounded his friend and found him quite ready to retire. From 1821 onwards he had no public life; he was primarily a cloth-worker, with a gradually growing taste for land (in 1820 he had about 4000 acres, by 1830 about 22,000), and found in those interests enough to occupy a full life and establish a family. One of his sons sat in one or the other branch of the colonial legislature almost continuously from 1843 to 1892, another from 1856 to 1880; the second was for eighteen months a Minister of the Crown. Simeon himself had died long before this, on 29 January, 1840.

Simeon Lord

A remarkable man, however you view him. One thing only obliterated the greater part of his original work. He lived in times when the colony was still small, and the full utilisation of its limited resources was the problem to be solved. All his experiments tended that way, towards the exploitation of its timbers and its farm products and its still scanty wool crop. But with the opening up of the vast inland areas, and the improvement in wool quality, and the influx of young gentry longing to become "squatters," Lord's experiments lost importance. Wool was king; what did wattle-bark and pearl-fishing and the making of blankets and hats locally matter to men who were running sheep by the hundred thousand and exporting wool by the thousand tons? For more than fifty years after Lord's death—until the droughts of the 1890's—wool, with its high intrinsic value and its low labour costs, dominated Australia's commerce and finance, and relegated the exploitation of her other resources to the rank of minor and rather fantastic enterprise. Lord, therefore, never came into his own. That lessens his importance, but not his greatness. He may not have been the absolute originator of the enterprises he fostered; the Blaxlands may have given him the flax-growing suggestion, Hutchison the cloth-making machine, Kent and Hutchison the notion to utilise wattle-bark. It was he who took the suggestions up, spent his money to try them out, returned again and again to them as new opportunities occurred. He was, one might say, the Henry Parkes of early Australian industry, the absorber of ideas, the practical enthusiast, the driving-power behind them. Born in these days, he would have become a millionaire and a peer of the realm. Born one hundred and fifty years ago, he was an emancipist, uncultured and despised—but a friend of Macquarie and a builder of Australia.

FRANCIS HOWARD GREENWAY

MACQUARIE'S second swan among the emancipists was Francis Howard Greenway. Of his early life we know only that he was born in 1777 and trained to be an architect, and that his practice lay chiefly in the West of England, especially in Bristol and Bath. He was also a student of what nowadays is called town-planning and landscape-gardening, and in the course of his work at Bath made the acquaintance of Arthur Phillip, who had been the founder of the settlement on Port Jackson but was, when Greenway met him, living on a pension in the outskirts of the famous spa. Neither architecture, however, nor town-planning brought him prosperity; in 1811 he was made bankrupt, and for concealing his effects on that occasion was in 1812 sentenced[1] to transportation for fourteen years. Now Phillip had himself been something of a town-planner—if Sydney had been permanently established on the plans he devised for it, the streets would have been two hundred feet wide at any rate, even if they had been also rather steep in places. When Phillip left Australia in 1792, his plans were pigeon-holed by the military Lieutenant-Governor who succeeded him, and for streets the town was given only bullock-tracks that wandered as best they might round the fences put up at random by officers looking for good garden ground. The old Governor never forgave this; and when he heard that Greenway was going to New South Wales, even as a convict, he wrote to the latest Governor, Macquarie, recommending

[1] Greenway was lucky; as late as 1807 a bankrupt was hanged for the same offence.

him to take the chance of getting expert advice on the reshaping of the marred township. Macquarie was not slow to take the chance. Greenway reached Port Jackson on 7 February, 1814; almost immediately he was granted a ticket-of-leave, and in July he was already providing at Macquarie's request a design for a market-house and town-hall (he was also copying, by order, a plan of some building of the Governor's own designing, and—for he was a conscientious artist with high ideals—objecting to it as "a building that has no claim to classical proportion or character"). In 1815 he launched out into more ambitious proposals. In the town itself the most important work—the new hospital—was already under construction by private contract; Greenway began with the approaches from seaward, advising the erection of a lighthouse on North Head, a beacon and fort on the Sow and Pigs reef just round the corner within the projecting guard of South Head, and—should a bold enemy manage to run the gauntlet of this fort—a strong fortress on the ridge west of Sydney Cove with a redoubt in front of it on the jutting point (Dawes Point) of the cove itself. Glancing into the future, he even envisaged a bridge from this point across the mile of tidal stream that separates Sydney from the northern shore of Port Jackson—a vision that is only now (1928) on the way to realisation. On the land side there was to be a wall, running in a flat curve from the head of Woolloomooloo Bay to that of Cockle Bay; and to provide a stately entrance for visiting ships the irregular bight of Sydney Cove was to be rounded off with a semi-circular stone quay at which the biggest vessels might lie and take in water from a pipe. Macquarie, a visionary himself as regarded the settlement, could not rise to those heights. He agreed in principle, but ordained that the lighthouse should

PLAN OF
SYDNEY
1823.

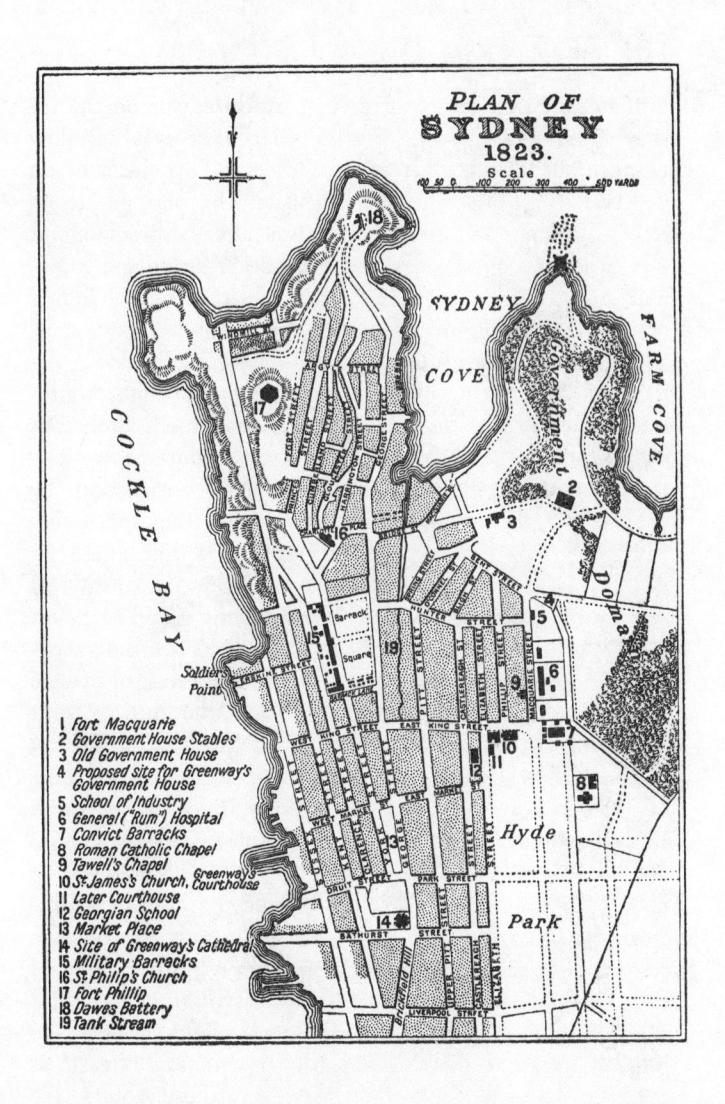

Scale
100 50 0 100 200 300 400 500 YARDS

SYDNEY COVE

FARM COVE

COCKLE BAY

Government

Domain

Hyde Park

1 Fort Macquarie
2 Government House Stables
3 Old Government House
4 Proposed site for Greenway's Government House
5 School of Industry
6 General ("Rum") Hospital
7 Convict Barracks
8 Roman Catholic Chapel
9 Tawell's Chapel
10 St. James's Church, Greenway's Courthouse
11 Later Courthouse
12 Georgian School
13 Market Place
14 Site of Greenway's Cathedral
15 Military Barracks
16 St. Philip's Church
17 Fort Phillip
18 Dawes Battery
19 Tank Stream

be set on South Head—where it could be reached by land from the town—and the fort (to be named after himself) on the eastern point of the cove. The fortress he postponed for lack of cash, though he was still contemplating its erection in 1820; the bridge and wall and quay he ignored altogether. Greenway yielded—he could do nothing else—but scored a cheerful repartee against his master; when his plans for Fort Macquarie were complete and under the Governor's inspection, he called particular attention to his *chef d'œuvre*, a great underground chamber. "Eh, what's that for?" said Macquarie. "That" said Greenway, "I propose to fill with gunpowder. Then, when the enemy captures your fort, as he certainly will without much trouble, you will be able to blow him sky-high." To his equals Greenway was less indirect; "I must confess" he wrote, "these fortification works put me in mind of My Uncle Toby and Corporal Trim in the garden."

On 16 April, 1816, Macquarie made him Colonial Architect, partly to give him status in checking over-expenditure on the private contracts. His experience soon proved useful; he found that two-thirds of the bricks supplied for buildings at Windsor were badly baked, and at Parramatta the jail, factory and orphan school were all prematurely dilapidated and the piers of the bridge falling to pieces. His constructive work, too, was of great value, and has stood the test both of time and of criticism; several of his churches and public buildings are still in use, and the demolition of a school built by him proved in 1923 a difficult and expensive business, although its material was almost entirely brick. On 16 December, 1817, to celebrate the completion of the lighthouse and the commencement of Fort Macquarie, Greenway was emancipated, and was encouraged again to bold flights of design. He proposed to decorate the eastern ridge above Sydney Cove with a Government House on the model of Thornbury Castle[1] in Gloucestershire, "only much bolder." Below the site chosen for it he built stables so majestic that a London illustrated newspaper reproduced their picture as one of Government House itself. Higher still along the same ridge the new "rum" hospital already stood; Greenway erected just beyond it convicts' barracks that are still—in spite of later excrescences and aggregations —admired specimens of sound Georgian building, and are utilised as minor law courts and public offices. Across the road he planned a new Court-house, "in the Ionic order, with a portico 40 feet high like that of the Temple of Minerva"; the two buildings would be connected (so that men held for trial could be brought to court under cover) by "a screen of the Doric order, which would correspond with a Doric Colonnade Aræostyle"[2] leading to the judges' chambers.

The western ridge, beyond the Tank Stream, was already occupied by military barracks and the beginnings of Fort Phillip (where the fortress should have stood); but at its root he planned a Circus with a Cathedral in the centre— like Wren's plan for St. Paul's—and roads that ran from its cardinal points south towards Parramatta, east into Hyde Park, north towards Fort Phillip, and west to Cockle Bay

---

[1] Thornbury Castle, built in 1511 by a Duke of Buckingham, was one of the glories of English domestic architecture. "The magnificent remains," writes a recent contributor to the county's history, "sufficiently denote the great spirit of both master and architect. . . . It is a happy specimen of the last gradation of Gothic architecture in the application of that style to castellated houses. Hampton Court is less rich." The west front resembled that of Christ Church College at Oxford. Greenway was certainly ambitious if he desired anything bolder.

[2] "Aræostyle," having columns four or more diameters apart —if that is any help.

(now Darling Harbour); a large fresh-water conduit intended to supply the whole town was to have a branch running down to this bay, so that vessels could water without trouble. A main town sewer was also among his projects; and—remembering, perhaps, Phillip's mistake—he warned Macquarie earnestly not to plan all his improvements as if the ground were entirely level.

The years from 1816 to 1819 were, no doubt, the happiest of Greenway's life; his visions ran riot, his work was sound, and his superior authority sympathised with him. A letter of 1819, written by Macquarie to the Colonial Office, is probably unique in its method of notifying obedience to orders:

> The allowance of 3s. per diem paid to Mr. Greenway I shall not fail to discontinue in Compliance with Your Lordship's Commands, as soon as the Services of that Officer Can possibly be dispensed with. . . . The Government Buildings Erected by him are not only Strong, durable and Substantial, but also Elegant and good Models of Architecture. I therefore respectfully Solicit that I may be Authorised by Your Lordship to increase Mr. Greenway's Salary to Five Shillings per diem.

It is, to say the least, unusual to acquiesce in the withdrawal of an employee's salary and in the same breath request that it should be raised.

In September of 1819, however, arrived Mr. John Thomas Bigge, of whom enough has been said in connection with Macquarie. Before the month was out the eager and confiding Greenway had explained to the new-comer his designs for the new Court-house and its approaches by Screen and Colonnade. Bigge, possibly overwhelmed for the moment, seemed to approve, and the foundation-stone was laid in his presence early in October. Much heartened, Greenway next sprang upon him the Cathedral and Circus, on which work had begun. Bigge began to think. This man was one of the Governor's pet emancipists, he remembered; it seemed that money was being spent like water (an unjust suspicion, for Greenway's work cost the country much less than the private contracts had); in any case, what had convicts to do with Doric colonnades and aræostyles? "The way you are going on," he told the expectant architect, "you'll make the place a finer city, architecturally, than London"; and to define his meaning he at once vetoed the cathedral, the colonnade, and the conduit, and insisted that the new court-house should be turned into a church—"expecting," says Greenway, "to hear a sermon preached in it before he quitted the colony by his worthy Reverend Adviser." For Marsden and Greenway were at daggers drawn already over the design for the cathedral; "I was bred a Churchman," protested the indignant architect, "and have designed a metropolitan church according to the principles of the Church of England, and not a Methodist chapel."

Bigge had his way. The cathedral waited seventeen years for a commencement and thirty-one more for completion. The court-house lost its Ionic portico and Doric colonnade, and became a church with a gallery full of convicts and services conducted (except when the Communion-table was actually in use) entirely from the middle of the southern wall. The "bolder than Thornbury Castle" design that was to have been Government House was peremptorily vetoed by Bathurst, who knew Thornbury well and saw no reason why British money should be squandered on reproducing it at Port Jackson. A "Georgian School" that Macquarie had sanctioned during Bigge's absence in Tasmania was at his return condemned as a school and converted into a temporary court-house. So one after the other all Greenway's dreams were dashed, and—to embitter the blow still more acridly—Macquarie withdrew his active support, and now acquiesced without a protest when orders from the Colonial Office abolished the architect's post and assigned a very meagre compensation for his past services. There were angry scenes at Government House. Greenway withdrew sullenly into private practice. The house he lived in, which had been promised to him as his personal property by Macquarie (unfortunately the promise was never put into writing), was taken back by Macquarie's successor as Government property. Fragments of his great designs—e.g. the semi-circular wharf on Sydney Cove that is now Circular Quay—were resuscitated by later officials and claimed as their own proposals. He may, if he ever saw Bigge's official reports, have derived a little compensatory pleasure from that gentleman's belated recognition of his merit:

Mr. Greenway's architectural skill has been the means of introducing into the buildings of the colony greater celerity and better taste than had previously prevailed. The ornamental style in which some of them have been finished cannot in fairness be made ground of charge against Mr. Greenway.

Other references in the reports mentioned "the valuable services of Mr. Greenway" and admitted that "the benefits derived from them have been very conspicuous." But belated praise at the other end of the world does not adequately support life. Greenway's private practice was not large— there were few men in the colony rich enough to afford buildings with any architectural character about them; but he struggled on, and spent his enforced leisure moments in writing to the newspapers. Thus in the early months of 1825 he contributed to the *Australian* (W. C. Wentworth's new venture, which was always ready to accept matter reflecting on officialdom) a series of letters detailing his work under Macquarie, and in 1834 the *Sydney Gazette* published his account of the originally projected harbour defences. By the next year he was in great trouble, and was compelled to make a public appeal for help:

> Francis Howard Greenway, Architect, Arising from circumstances of a singular nature, is induced again to solicit the patronage of his Friends and the Public.

In May 1837 he was eager to obtain formal possession of a block of land near Morpeth on the Hunter River, which had been promised him by Macquarie (this time in writing); the long delay in claiming it possibly indicates that he had at last given up hope of supporting himself by his profession, and was expecting to turn farmer at the age of sixty. Before the claim could be granted — as it eventually was — the claimant was dead, when and how we know not. Our only record shows that on 25 September he was buried at Maitland, a few miles from Morpeth, by the parish schoolmaster, the local chaplain being away on leave.

So disappears Australia's first great artist. The meagre story of his life here told—and, unless his private letters still exist in some old family chest at Grafton (where a son of his was archdeacon), the story will remain meagre—cannot do him justice, and will probably interest only those who, living in New South Wales, can see some of the buildings he erected and the localities he proposed to adorn. But a great artist he was, after his fashion; and it was he alone, except for Macquarie's backing (which is assuredly a feather in Macquarie's bonnet), who rescued the young colony from drab Philistinism and made it impossible to bury completely one of the world's noblest city sites under a hotch-potch of wattle and dab, or poor bricks and worse cast-iron, huddled along narrow streets and sprawling over the long peninsular ridges.

GEORGE HOWE

To St. Kitts in the West Indies—the third oldest colony of the Empire, that has been British for three hundred years and more—there came when the Seven Years War was over a roving Irishman with a printing-press. Settling down there to print General Orders and Port Regulations for the local Government, he soon found himself in a turmoil of politics roused by the Stamp Act of 1765; for St. Kitts was as much disturbed over that foolish piece of legislation as its neighbours on the mainland to the north-west, and might easily have become the Massachusetts of the West Indies had it found among them another Vermont or Virginia. Richard Howe must have been suspected of sharing the general discontent, but managed to clear himself and to retain the Government printing; and, when in 1769 he had a son to baptise, he felt it wise to show his loyalty by naming the boy George.

George, however, inherited his father's discontent, and when he came of age proceeded to discuss local and British politics unguardedly and unfavourably. Soon he found it best to migrate to London, where he obtained work as a printer's assistant and in a year or so was taken on at Printing House Square itself. No one knows what happened next, but the solid anti-Jacobinism of *The Times* disagreed with his digestion somehow, and in 1800 George Happy was sent off to New South Wales on a seven-years' sentence and re-metamorphosed himself on arrival at Port Jackson into George Howe. Governor Hunter, whose official printer had just completed his sentence and departed for

England, reckoned himself a favourite of Providence, and at once requisitioned Howe to fill the vacant place—for his bare board. King, finding the recruit skilful and intelligent, gave him a definite salary, and in 1802 Howe published the first book known to have been printed in Australia. Widely read though it was, and valuable though it is to-day, it was neither of literary nor of sensational quality; it was merely

New South Wales General Standing Orders: selection from the General Orders issued by Former Governors from the 16th of February, 1791, to the 6th of September, 1800. Also, General Orders issued by Governor King from the 28th of September, 1800, to the 30th of September, 1802.
Sydney: Printed at Government Press, 1802.

King was so pleased with this firstling that Howe persuaded him into approval of a more daring venture. Why wait several years, he said, for a collection of General Orders? Why not print them as they came along—in a real newspaper? King agreed; and on 5 May, 1803, there appeared the first issue of the *Sydney Gazette and New South Wales Advertiser*. King's purpose was patent on the face of it: "All Advertisements, Orders, etc., which appear . . . in the *Sydney Gazette and New South Wales Advertiser* are meant, and must be deemed to convey official and sufficient Notifications." Howe's purpose was there, too, tucked away underneath three General Orders:

The utility of a *Paper* in the *Colony*, as it must open a source of solid information, will, we hope, be universally felt and acknowledged. We have courted the assistance of the Ingenious and Intelligent:—We open no channel to Political Discussion, or Personal Animadversion:—Information is our only Purpose; that accomplished, we shall consider that we have done our duty, in an exertion to merit the Approbation of the *Public*, and to secure a liberal Patronage to the *Sydney Gazette*.

The first advertisement followed—John Jaques, tailor, announced "an abatement in his charges" on account of "the reduction that has lately taken place in the Prices of many Articles of common Consumption." Sound economics, no doubt, but not usually so plainly set forth.

Howe's venture was for some years the most casual, haphazard and kaleidoscopic newspaper the world has ever seen. He invited contributions by means of two "slip boxes," one placed in front of the public "issuing" store at Sydney, the other in a window of the Parramatta Court-house. But the trap was set almost in vain. Howe himself had to write —or compile—most of the matter, a serious task whenever King took a rest from General Orders; he had also to set and distribute the type, print the issue, and deliver their copies to subscribers week by week. No—not week by week; the *Gazette* was not as punctual as all that. It appeared when it could and how it could; sometimes it was a four-page foolscap issue, sometimes two pages on a half-sheet of demy; its colours, Howe wrote reminiscently in later years, rivalled the chameleon's, and its shapes were Protean. The ink, however, was uniformly bad, the type worn, and the printing-machine overworked into a premature old age. At the beginning of 1805 he was advertising anxiously for paper:

WANTED TO PURCHASE, any quantity of Demy, Medium, folio Post, or Foolscap PAPER, for the use of Printing; and which, if from any accident from damp or slight mildew rendered unfit for writing, will answer the purpose.

At that time he was ready to pay cash, but worse days were to come. Up to the June of 1806 he was still technically a convict serving his sentence, and could draw Government rations. On the 4th of that month, however, King graciously but with a certain lack of consideration issued him a full pardon—and threw him entirely on his own resources. He had already attempted to obtain more cash by publishing a *Pocket Almanac* for 1806, but only a fragment of it was ready by January and he was still apologising for its incompleteness in May. In March he opened a stationery shop; in November he made a new departure and opened an evening school. Arithmetic and mensuration were his staple subjects, but he was willing to teach writing if necessary, and for really zealous students had wider fields of study:

> The Grammar of the English Tongue upon the Principles of Drs. Lowth, Johnson, Priestly, and other celebrated writers who have united their efforts in improving the Grammatical structure of their own beautiful and comprehensive Language, which every Englishman ought to be acquainted with, but few attain, that have not had the advantage of a classical education.

One wonders where Howe got his classical education.

Under the Bligh régime his affairs worsened rapidly. Between April and August of 1807 he missed five weeks' issues, and on 30 August the *Gazette* suspended publication, nominally for lack of paper, but probably for lack of cash to buy it with. Not till some months after the Bligh mutiny, when in May 1808 John Macarthur found it imperative to resuscitate the one satisfactory medium of communication with outlying settlements (the Hawkesbury was still strongly pro-Bligh, and had to be impressed somehow with the permanence of the new rule), could Howe set his press running again. In 1809 the arrears of subscriptions began to give him trouble, and Colonel Foveaux, who had taken over the administration of affairs, issued a General Order advising recalcitrants to pay up and offering to buy corn from them at any public store up to the value of their debt to Howe. The same year Howe enlarged his school by the addition of an infant department, in which he offered for five guineas each to teach six children in four months "from the Alphabet to read the Testament, as correctly as the weakness of childhood will admit." But pedagogy proved too distracting a side-line, and at the beginning of 1810 he abandoned it and threw himself heart and soul into re-establishing his newspaper. To begin with, he endeavoured to collect overdue subscriptions, politely at first, then with elaborate insistence. On 12 April he pleaded:

> The mortifying embarrassments in which the Publisher of this Paper is involved, by the Non-payment of Subscriptions, unfortunately affords him another opportunity of animadverting on the excessive inattention[1] which has at length fallen with extreme severity upon him. Labouring under reflexions at the present moment from which everything pleasant is alienated,

he went on to warn his debtors that, unless they paid up within a fortnight, those more than twelve months behind would find their names and the amount of their arrears published;

and if this method also fail, the further supply will cease, and a less delicate mode resorted to for attracting the attention of the negligent.

In May, discovering that the less delicate mode was becoming imperative, he had a brilliant idea. He became a professional debt-collector, thus recovering without added expense the amounts owed to himself and earning a small commission on the amounts recovered for other people while on his rounds. His abandonment of educational work was compensated, as far as concerned the colony's interests, partly by Macquarie's foundation of a free school in Sydney, partly by the arrival of, one fears, an unworthy successor.

[1] "Animadverting on the excessive inattention"! May we trace in this and similar phrases some faint scent of the roses he had plucked ten years before in Printing House Square?

Mr. T. Macqueen, in spite of a boasted thirty years' experience, and "a knowledge of the latin classics," proposed to teach "the English language, agreeable to the modern pronunciation, and grammattically, if required." One would have liked to hear one of the lessons given to pupils who did not require it.

Better times were close at hand. But before we pass on to them, we may consider two stories that belong to the lean years—one purely comic, the other of serious import and almost destructive of the colony's legal existence. The comic incident was a by-product of the Bligh mutiny. Howe's printing-office was merely a shanty built up against the side of Government House, with a loft above it where he stored his paper and oddments. When Colonel Johnston let loose his eager troops to hunt down Governor Bligh—who had retired to an upper room in the main building to hide or destroy some official papers—some of the rebel officers took it into their heads that Howe was concealing the Governor in the store-loft. Up went Lieutenant Laycock in full uniform through a very inadequate man-hole; busily he rummaged among piles of newsprint and kegs of ink and packages of mildewed, unsold *Gazettes*; and Howe relates with malicious glee how, baffled and filthy and hot with rage, the officer struggled back through the man-hole and fell all of a heap into the main shanty, nearly dislocating the principal joints in his body.

The other is not so much an incident as a long-drawn-out catastrophe. In November 1823 James Stephen—legal adviser to the Colonial Office—answering an inquiry about the law applicable to the registration of mortgages in Tasmania, bluntly replied:

"There are reasons why it might be inconvenient to pledge yourself to any point respecting the law of this settlement. In my opinion they have no law at all which can properly be recognised as such." This was, indirectly and unconsciously, Howe's doing. For under the original ordinances constituting the colony of New South Wales the General Orders issued by Governors had no permanent legal force unless they were confirmed by the Colonial Office; Hunter or King made the Order, and it had to be obeyed there and then, but was merely provisional till some authority in London had countersigned it. The process was usually almost mechanical; the Governor's secretary sent home beautifully engrossed copies by each mail, and was notified by a subsequent return mail that everything was in order. As this notification could not arrive for more than a year, it was regarded in the colony as a mere formality, and no one grew anxious if it did not turn up—if the Colonial Office had any objections to the Orders, it had quicker and more unpleasant ways of notifying them. All went well until 1803, when, as we have seen, King and Howe between them devised the *Gazette* as a handier way of promulgating Orders than the old fashion of hand-copying them. They appeared in print in the *Gazette*, and the secretary in due course forwarded to London copies of the *Gazette* for confirmation. But this was outside Colonial Office routine. A written document was something that demanded attention, and received it. These badly printed newspapers — what were they? why should oversea Governors load up the Office mails with matter of that sort? (The Office, we must remember, was just then occupied with the war as well as with the colonies, and its staff had no time to work their way through ephemeral journalism from Port Jackson.) So the *Gazettes* were pigeon-holed as they came along; and no official seems to have noticed the lack of New South Wales General Orders; and Bligh and Macquarie and Brisbane (or their secretaries) forwarded copies of the *Gazette* regularly, and did not trouble themselves because no acknowledgment was made. Probably neither Macquarie nor Brisbane so much as knew that acknowledgment and confirmation were needed. At any rate the Orders remained unconfirmed, and New South Wales for twenty years carried on under an illegal régime, and nobody was a penny the worse, until Stephen woke up with a shock to the fact that the colony had no law at all—"as far as I am aware, the laws of New South Wales have never been transmitted for confirmation at home," he wrote, his legal and precise intelligence being as yet unable to grasp the uses of press publication.

Meanwhile Howe, never suspecting the consternation he was some day to rouse in the Colonial Office, struggled bravely on. His issues for 1810 rarely exceeded two pages, and their contents were chiefly advertisements. But in 1811 Macquarie woke up to the value of his work, and procured for him both a steady supply of paper and a salaried appointment as Government Printer. Purely from the official point of view it was very advantageous, now that the colony was expanding and small isolated settlements were springing up in out-of-the-way patches of bushland, to have ready to hand a means of easy distribution for Government orders and announcements. Howe prospered now as never before; he became almost a capitalist, married a rich widow, put his savings (and hers) into speculations in sandalwood trading, and in 1817 was wealthy enough to be one of the original founders of the Bank of New South Wales. Then, of a sudden, his prosperity crashed about his ears. In 1818 the *Gazette*, which had for many years fitted tightly into four pages, found itself unable to pad out more than two, and the other two in some issues were left blank. In 1819 his old trouble—subscribers who would not pay up—beset him once more. He let his eloquence loose again, implored the public not to let him "take his whity-brown locks with sorrow to the grave," announced that out of three hundred clients half were badly in arrears, and sent out the overdue accounts as "a Christmas-box." One cannot but admire his humour as well as his pluck. In January 1821 he was still alert enough to stand cross-examination by Commissioner Bigge, though his memory was obviously failing. But dropsy afflicted him beyond endurance, and on 11 May he died. His son Robert, who had shared the *Gazette's* troubles since its inception, carried on the business—in spite of several libel actions, a horsewhipping, and an attempt at assassination—until he was drowned in 1829; another son, George Terry, was for a time Government Printer in Tasmania and editor of the *Tasmanian Gazette* (usually known as the *Tasmanian*). And all the while the family in St. Kitts was pursuing its ancestral occupation undisturbedly. If journalism benefits a community at all, the Howes deserved well of the Empire.

As for George, no monument adorned his grave. But in his printing-office (and he would probably have preferred that place) his son put up a marble memorial that, inadequately perhaps but with attention to essentials, records this:

In Memory of George Howe, a Creole, of Saint Kitts; born 1769, died May 11th, 1821, Aged 52. He Introduced into Australia the Art of Printing; Instituted the *Sydney Gazette*; And was the First Government Printer. Besides which, His Charity Knew No Bounds.

Greater men have lacked so noble an epitaph.

WILLIAM HILTON HOVELL

AMONG the pioneers of Australian exploration none has been more misjudged and undervalued than William Hovell, the partner of Hamilton Hume in the first overland journey between Sydney and Port Phillip. The reasons for his undervaluation will be discussed later; our first business is to understand the man himself and the salient points of his career.

Born at Yarmouth in Norfolk on 26 April, 1786, William Hovell at the age of ten went to sea in a fishing-smack and within twelve years had pushed his way up to the command of a vessel trading with South America. He was not, however, a mariner born, and tired early of voyaging (although he was always proud of his seamanship); but he was adventurous on general principles, and if the sea bored him England bored him too. By 1812 he had married—how, we know not, for the family into which he married had been brought up, and still lived, in Australia—the daughter of a medical man who had accompanied Phillip to New South Wales in 1788, and after retiring from the profession had settled down as a farmer there. Probably at his wife's instigation Hovell determined to try New South Wales himself as a field for adventures, obtained from the Colonial Office the usual recommendation as a desirable settler—the desirability consisted chiefly in the fact that he was able to take with him at least £500 worth of marketable goods—and in October 1813 reached Port Jackson, where in his endeavours to dispose of his merchandise he made the acquaintance of the auctioneer Simeon Lord, then much occupied with his scheme for exploiting New Zealand trade. A master mariner with a love of adventure was very welcome just then, and before Hovell quite knew what he was about he found himself a working partner in Lord's "New Zealand Trading Company." For various reasons (set out on pp. 171–2 above) the company never took definite shape, but Lord and Hovell carried on undiscouraged. Hovell as master of the *Trial* (which has given its name to Trial Bay in northern New South Wales) made trading trips to New Zealand and along the Australian coast north and south; an encounter with the Maoris at Kennedy Bay put a stop to the New Zealand branch of the enterprise, and Lord gave him the *Brothers* for a voyage to Port Dalrymple in northern Tasmania, but this venture ended in shipwreck on the Kent group of Bass Strait Islands. Another venture, concerned with the sealing off Kangaroo Island—a real venture, this, for the sealers in those southern waters had a reputation that would have disgraced West Indian buccaneers—brought Hovell information that might, if he had thought well over it, have given him the glory that was to be Sturt's; a friendly sealer, chatting over his sea wanderings, mentioned that away eastward in the great bight of Encounter Bay one could sight from the mast-head a long stretch of lagoon behind the coastal sandhills, and at its northern end what looked like a big river flowing into it.

But, as has been already said, Hovell was not really enamoured of the sea. The most vital trait of marinership in him was his desire to become a farmer; and in 1819 he severed partnership with Lord, settled on a block of land south-west of Sydney that he had three years before secured for this purpose, and—finding his farming as wearisome as his voyaging—promptly entered on a series of minor explorations in the rough foothill country to southwards, where through barren sandstone plateaux and sudden precipitous gorges that intersected them one could often light upon fine areas of cattle-pasture. In 1823 he discovered in a previously neglected section of the Blue Mountain area a splendid well-watered valley (the Burragorang valley), access to which was only obtainable by cliff-climbing, but was well worth the trouble. It may have been this discovery which brought him into close contact with Governor Brisbane, though his status was quite good enough to make him without any special reason a welcome guest of the old astronomer; at any rate Brisbane rewarded him for his new valley with another land-grant, and took him into consultation over a proposed revival of exploration inland. Possibly influenced[1] by Hovell's story of the Kangaroo Island sealer's mysterious lagoon and the big river that fed it, Brisbane conceived the idea of an expedition due west across country towards Spencer Gulf, where a vessel might await its arrival; unfortunately, however, he found himself unable to spare from the colonial treasury—which was much more carefully supervised than it had been in Macquarie's time—any substantial help for the equipment of the expedition. Nor did Hovell (who never overvalued his own brains) feel himself competent, on the strength of a few excursions into coastal country covering a few hundred miles at most, to take charge of an exploration that must penetrate seven or eight hundred miles of absolutely unknown inland wastes.

In the circumstances Brisbane consulted one Alexander Berry, who had travelled out with him (in Berry's own

[1] Brisbane gave the river as his reason; he wrote to the Colonial Office: "They were directed by me to try and reach Spencer's Gulf, in the hope of intercepting any Rivers that might run South to that parallel of longitude, and discharge themselves into these Streights."

vessel) and was already a prosperous merchant and a daring coastal explorer; and Berry strongly recommended the employment of young Hamilton Hume, who had for ten years—though at this time still only twenty-seven—been opening up odd corners of the southern bushland and convoying cattle and sheep to the new pastures. Brisbane saw that the conjunction of Hume's expert bushmanship with Hovell's scientific knowledge and experience of the world might make history; he brought the two together, and revived for them the proposal to open an overland route to Spencer Gulf. Hume would have dared the venture willingly, but could not raise the necessary funds. He talked the matter over with Hovell, and the two came back to Brisbane with a counter-proposal that was within their means — a cross-country expedition towards Western Port, exactly reversing the suggestion made by Bigge a little earlier that an expedition should be sent from the shores of Bass Strait in the direction of Lake George. Simple as the proposal may seem to-day, it was daring enough in those days; Surveyor-General Oxley, himself an explorer of no mean grade, declared:

We had demonstrated beyond a doubt . . . that the country south of the parallel of $34°$ S., and east of the meridian $147° 30'$ E., was uninhabitable and useless for all the purposes of civilised man.

Brisbane agreed to "sanction" this proposal, and contributed from Government stores some pack-saddles, muskets and ammunition, clothes and blankets for the convicts who were to accompany the explorers, and a tent; otherwise the whole expense was borne equally by the two, each bringing along three convict servants and providing 640 lb. flour, 200 lb. pork, 100 lb. sugar, and tea, tobacco, soap, salt, coffee, etc., in suitable quantities. A mysterious instrument which is listed among the supplies as "one perambulator" was really a measuring-wheel which one of the convicts had to run along in front of him over the track, so as to get a rough notion of the distance travelled; when it broke down in the far southern bush, it was dignified at burial with the new names "odimeter" and "Hodometer."

Hume had a station on the limits of settlement at Lake George, and was well acquainted with the type of country in that direction. It was therefore decided that they should start from the lake and make as nearly as possible southwest to Western Port; Port Phillip as a destination seems to have occurred to no one, Collins having given so unfavourable a report on it in 1803. On 17 October, 1824, they left the station, and after a day's journey through more or less known lands (Yass[1] Plains, which they re-named "McDougall's" after the Governor's second patronymic) plunged into a tangle of deep rocky gullies that drained into the Murrumbidgee. Lake George, as a glance at the map will show, was an ideally bad spot from which to start for Bass Strait. Hovell's instinct served him well, but too late, when it prompted him to say to Hume, "We should have done far better to start from Bathurst"; the mileage would have been greater, but the country far more traversable,[2] and nine-tenths of their hardships would have been avoided. The story of their journey has often been told—unfortunately with stupid legendary additions that will be referred to later on. Here we may note only the critical moments, such as that when, after waiting for three days on the banks

[1] "Yass" is merely a corruption of the aboriginal Yarrh, "running water," from which also comes the name of Melbourne's Yarra.

[2] The old main road from Sydney to Melbourne still follows roughly in the Hume-Hovell tracks, but the more cautious railway line runs west from Goulburn to reach as quickly as possible the easier country along the Bathurst-Albury route.

of the flooded Murrumbidgee, they took a cart off its wheels, wrapped it round with a strong tarpaulin, and used it for a punt in which to cross the six-miles-an-hour, 150-feet-wide current. Hume—who throughout was admittedly the best bushman, the deviser of expedients, and the discoverer of passable tracks through scarcely penetrable country—swam the river first with a tow-line, and in five hours men and stores and cattle and horses were safe across, though one of the bullocks was dragged over upside down, with only its hooves showing above the stream. Then for nearly a month they wandered in a maze of gorges and precipitous hills, always trying to get away from the Murrumbidgee, again and again forced back to it by "an almost perpendicular range" or "a mountain chasm not more than ten feet wide," or a native track just wide enough for one man, with the rapid stream fifteen feet below, and above "the mountain, inclining not more than 15 or 20 degrees from the perpendicular." This obstacle compelled them on 27 October to abandon the carts and pack their stores on the bullocks, which the weather as well as the toil affected gravely ("Thermometer at sunrise 50°; at noon 89° in the tent"). On 8 November, while scouting ahead to find a practicable track, the two explorers "were suddenly surprised by a sight to the utmost degree magnificent. Mountains of a conoidal form and of an apparently immense height, and some of them covered about one-fourth of their height with snow," extended in a semi-circle along the south-eastern horizon under a bright sun. So exciting was the display that Hume called to the convicts in the valley behind, and they came scrambling up the hillside to admire the Australian Alps. The sight was useful as well as pleasing, for it warned them off the southern route which they were trying to pursue. For some days they made west and north, crossing more ravines with the aid of kangaroo-tracks, but emerging at last into open forest watered by chains of ponds, and, as they again turned south, reaching on 16 November a fine river running in a bed two hundred and fifty feet wide between a perpetual succession of lagoons. This they named the Hume.[1] Skirting the lagoons first downwards and then up stream, it took them four days to find a crossing-place; but they were still too far east for easy going, and repeatedly climbed and descended transverse ranges which ten miles to westward lapsed into grassy plains. A little way beyond the Goulburn-Hovell, which they reached on 3 December, they entangled themselves in impenetrable scrub. For a time they had to encamp the convicts and the cattle and work forward by themselves, their task not made easier by bush-fires; at last they found a way through, descended into a huge treeless plain, and on the 16th were "struck with an appearance respecting which we cannot decide whether it is that of burning grass

[1] The nomenclature of this journey is a puzzle. In this case Hovell says he named the river "Hume" after his companion, who was the first to see it; Hume, thirty years later, said *he* named it "Hume" after his father. A river found later Hovell named "Goulburn" after the Governor's secretary. Hume first tried to get the name changed to "Hovell," and afterwards declared that Hovell had named it after himself and he, Hume, had insisted on "Goulburn." A third river, which Hume named "Arndell" after Hovell's father-in-law, lost its name altogether for some years, and is now known as the Maribyrnong.

The "Hume," of course, is the upper part of the Murray. Sturt, reaching it lower down its course, named it afresh because he did not know of any connection between them. It is a pity that the old name cannot be resuscitated—several Australian rivers have several names each, notably the Hawkesbury, which begins as the Wollondilly, and becomes Warragamba and Nepean before it acquires its final name.

or of distant water." Water it was—the wide, shallow expanse of Port Phillip—and they skirted its shores south-westwards to a point that jutted out into what is now Corio Bay.

And here Hovell made his crucial mistake. Port Phillip was never in his mind, nor in Hume's; they were expecting to find Western Port. Hovell, the ci-devant navigator, took observations and worked out the longitude—and made it 145° 25′, exactly one degree too far east. The story of Australian exploration has several moments of dramatic failure—Torres feeling his way through the straits, unconscious that fifty miles south of him was the continent he was sent to find; Carstensz driven by the trade-winds out of Endeavour Strait when he was within ten miles of his goal; later on, Sturt lying scorched and blinded on the edge of the stony desert, Burke and Wills turning miserably away from food and succour into the barren wilds towards Lake Eyre. But high among them must be reckoned the moment when Hovell and Hume stood on the edge of Port Phillip and took it for the useless and untamable Western Port, could not understand the aborigines who were telling them how Collins had camped just across the harbour (an infallible clue to their true position), and were prevented by distrust of those same natives from turning west, as they had intended, into the glorious volcanic pastures that have for ninety years now been the Eden of Victorian squatters.

They had seen enough, however, to know that the new-found land was "a fine dry sheep pasturage" and well worth colonising. And on the 18th they turned back, well content with themselves, to take home the good news. The return journey was slightly easier, because they traversed the slighter foothills west of their outward route—to-day's railway follows this second choice of theirs. But they were in too much of a hurry to divagate unnecessarily; they had not tasted meat since Christmas Day, the flour was almost exhausted, so were the cattle, the men's shoes were worn out, and they had to travel barefoot through a blazing summer—which at any rate dried up the rivers and made them fordable. On 8 January, 1825, each man received his last six pounds of flour, and from that time they had to live on fish, for their one dog was too weary to hunt down a kangaroo. On the 13th they shot one, however, and feasted, using the animal's skin (along with those of previous victims) to make moccasins for the cattle. On the 16th they reached the carts they had left behind more than eleven weeks earlier, and the starvation period was over. Two days later they were at Lake George.

The immediate results of this adventurous journey—which has lost most of its romantic glamour because the area which it opened up is now so well known and easily traversed—were disappointing. Certainly, the discovery of stream after stream that vanished west or north-west into the mysterious bush confirmed Brisbane in his belief that there was a great river somewhere in the Spencer Gulf direction to receive all those waters; but it also convinced him that his original orders had been right, and that Hume and Hovell had been foolish to substitute their own enterprise for his. Further, the one unmistakably valuable discovery had been that of the pasture-lands near "Western Port," so that one of the first acts of his successor, Governor Darling, was to organise an expedition by sea to occupy that inlet and establish a small settlement on the good lands. In 1826 the party set off in charge of a Captain Wright, Hovell being attached to it as explorer and guide; but it did not take long to discover that nowhere on Western Port lay the lands he had walked over, and when he worked round the top of the Port into the swamps north-west of it he found himself on the low cliffs that edge Port Phillip below St. Kilda—and saw thence across a wide expanse of shallows easily identified ridges, the You-Yangs and Anakies, rising from the long-sought pastures. Hovell it was who corrected his own mistake, and in the diary of this second exploration, written up night by night, his regretful entry of the error and its correction may be seen by any visitor to the Mitchell Library at Sydney. The news, however, reached Sydney too late; Darling was fully occupied with local troubles, sick of the Western Port scheme—which was admittedly a failure—and not at all inclined to waste money or thought on a new venture towards Port Phillip. After all, explorers who had made a bad mistake about its situation might be quite capable of making another about the excellence of its pasturages. Hovell for his part had by this time had a surfeit of adventure; he was over forty, and had a family to bring up; for a good many years the only records of him are connected with his attempts to obtain adequate recompense for the work he had done. In 1828 and 1829 he applied to Darling, in 1829 and 1830 he petitioned the Colonial Office. In 1833 he renewed his pleas to Bourke. In 1839 he appealed to the Colonial Office once more "for myself and Mr. Hamilton Hume." But Darling was for some unspecified reason distinctly hostile, and all that the generous Bourke could do was to cancel a debt he owed the Government for the use of convict labour on his farm; after all, the best Hovell could say was, "The area Mr. Hume and I found for you has since been proved by others to be of great value"—not a very convincing argument with which to bombard Downing Street.

Meanwhile other disturbances were brewing. The personal relations between Hovell and Hume seem never to have been really friendly. During the journey itself amicability was the rule; Hovell, according to his own diary and to a report of Sturt's, named the Hume, and certainly gave Hume again and again the credit of finding the right track and displaying expert bushmanship, while Hume (whose diary was of little value) at any rate named a river after Hovell's father-in-law and made one attempt to get Hovell's own name on the map. But Hume's friends had no use for his companion, and very soon after the return were doing their best to laud the young Australian in the press as the one man worth praise; "Mr. Hovell," said one advertisement, "lacks all the qualities befitting a Bush Ranger." When in 1831 William Bland at last published the *Journey of Discovery to Port Phillip*, and placed Hovell's name before Hume's on the title-page, he roused a storm, and had to explain that the precedence was due merely to the fact that Hume's journal had been almost useless to him and Hovell's had furnished the bulk of his matter. Hume himself, too, was touchy about his Australian birth; when writing to the Colonial Office about his services he must needs add "presuming myself (altho' an Australian) capable from experience of conducting such an expedition." The man who wrote that was looking for offence. In 1828 he went exploring with Sturt in the west; if we may believe the narrative compiled many years later by Mrs. Sturt from her husband's journals, even then he was disgruntled with Hovell and inclined to assume to himself the whole credit of the southern expedition. If anything can be made certain by a man's own written admissions, it is certain that Hume accepted without demur Hovell's belief that they had reached Western Port; he told Brisbane so the moment they reached Sydney, and in April 1826 demanded from the Colonial Office a grant of land at Western Port on the ground of his discovery of it. Yet in 1828 (if the Sturt journals may be trusted) he claimed that he had all along believed the pastures to be on Port Phillip; Hovell, of course, had discovered that the year before. After the Sturt expedition Hume retired to farm land near Yass, and sank into comparative obscurity. In 1853, however, the town of Geelong, which had sprung up near the spot where Port Phillip had been reached, invited the two to a banquet; Hume refused, Hovell went and in his speech gave Hume a full share of the credit. Unfortunately Melbourne reporters (as reporters will) cut down the speech considerably, and gave the impression that Hovell had claimed everything for himself. Hume, now aged before his time and admittedly cursed with a failing memory, burst into senile passion and attacked Hovell with bitter railing, raking up from the ex-convicts who had accompanied him and who were now his cronies spiteful stories tending to display the elder man as a coward, ignorant of all bush-craft and really a clog on the expedition. Hovell replied with as much dignity as he could muster, but the controversy that ensued would be better forgotten had not Hume's side of it managed to obtain acceptance as history. To this day school-children in New South Wales are taught how a bright and experienced young Australian outmanœuvred and put to shame the ignorant old mariner from England who had been foisted on him by Governor Brisbane.

Hovell was no ignorant old mariner. He belonged to an armour-bearing English family; he was well educated, always a welcome guest at the Governor's table; he met there, and formed personal friendships with, several French men of science who visited Port Jackson as members of Duperrey's expedition in January 1824; to one of them he sent the narrative of the journey printed in the *Australian* on 10

February, 1825, and it was translated for publication in the *Nouvelles Annales des Voyages* in December of that year. When he and Hume went off together, he was in the prime of life (thirty-seven) and Hume ten years younger; Hume was no doubt the better bushman, but Hovell was by far the more accomplished man.

Of his life there is little more to be said. The turmoil of the Hume attack died down after a year or two, and Hovell lived peaceably on his Narellan farm, too old to be concerned with politics—which were Sydney's sole diet in the 'sixties—until he died in 1875. Hume's death two years earlier had produced a recrudescence of the old quarrel, but on the other side only; it did not even stir Hovell's friends to hunt out the evidence on his side that was lying all the time among his own papers—and came to light at last in 1921. Nor was there any need for a recrudescence. The value of the work done—not only on the best-known journey, in which they shared, but on other exploring journeys and in other capacities—is not so small that either need grudge the other a share of it. Both were good Australians while they lived in Australia; the fact that Hume's whole life was spent there does not make him a better Australian, but only a narrower one. And Hovell, with whom we are more particularly concerned here, should be remembered also as an excellent specimen of those adventurous and adaptable Britons by whose gallant and arduous travels on land and sea the young coastal colonies of the Western Pacific gained both a more intimate knowledge of each other and a surer foothold on the vast, mysterious continent they clung to.

JAMES KING OF IRRAWANG

AMONG the more imaginative of the young adventurers who reached New South Wales in the late 1820's James King, usually known as King of Irrawang, deserves special notice. We know nothing about him, except that he came from Edinburgh, until he reached Port Jackson early in 1827, intending to establish himself in Sydney as a merchant, and found himself saddled with two thousand acres of not particularly fertile land on the Williams River, about thirty miles from Newcastle. On this estate he tried to grow wheat and breed cattle, both rather perfunctorily; his heart was in Sydney, among the traders and the shipping folk. But in 1831 his imagination woke up. To begin with, he discovered near Waterloo, on the road between Sydney and Botany Bay, huge deposits of a fine white sand, free from oxide of iron and other insoluble ingredients, which a reputable English firm of glass-blowers reported on as better suited for the manufacture of fine plate and flint glass than any at that time available in England. King promptly put in a memorial to Lord Goderich, then in charge of colonial affairs, urging the high value of this discovery; it would allow shipmasters to "ballast their vessels with an article worth 30s. per ton in place of taking on useless shingle . . . and, being heavier than the common ballast here, will enable the vessel to carry larger cargoes of wool and flax." Unfortunately King placed too high a value on his find, demanding a town allotment of fifty acres in or near Sydney; Goderich, ascertaining from other glass-blowers that the sand was all that was claimed for it, but the cost of carriage inland at the

English end would be prohibitive, hinted to Governor Bourke that King might be rewarded moderately. Bourke suggested £100, to be allowed off the price of any land he might care to purchase; too proud to accept so little, but partly consoled by the award of the Society of Arts' silver medal for his discovery, King shook off the dust of Sydney and retired to his farm at Irrawang on the Williams.

Here he initiated more profitable and more notable enterprises. The soil, he found, was unsuitable for wheat, so he built kilns along the river-bank and started the manufacture of pottery; by 1838 he was supplying Sydney with excellent brown earthenware. The slopes behind his river-flats he turned to still better use, making of them a viticultural laboratory in which he carried on persistent and methodical experiments. Vine-growing was not, literally speaking, a new industry for Australia. Gregory Blaxland, as we have seen, had been exporting samples of wine in the 1820's, and gaining silver and gold medals therefor; James Busby (afterwards the first British Resident in New Zealand) had published in Sydney in 1825 a *Treatise on the Culture of the Vine* and in 1830 a *Manual of Plain Directions*, also importing upwards of one thousand one hundred varieties of raisin-, dessert-, and wine-grapes from Spanish and French vineyards, most of which went to the Sydney botanic gardens. But King seems to have been unable to procure any satisfactory instruction when he in his turn commenced viticulturist; he had to discover for himself the best methods of training and pruning the vines, of locating the vineyards, of selecting the wine-grapes, of blending the juices [1] and

---

[1] In 1852 Von Liebig particularly commended "your proposal of mixing the must of the Verdeilho grape with the juice of the Gouais." It would be interesting to have a modern vigneron's opinion on the proposal.

mellowing the raw wines. For the most part he worked with stocks already grown in the colony; many importations from Spain, Portugal and France he found unsuited to the New South Wales climate, and a selection of stocks from the Rhine unfortunately died on the voyage out. In 1832 he planted his first vines, in 1836 he made the first wine from them. In course of time he "succeeded in producing a good marketable wine, the white resembling Hock or Sauterne, and the red wine that of Burgundy." The resemblance was probably vague to begin with.

In 1847 wine-making took a sudden spurt in New South Wales. King had never lacked competitors—among others Henry J. Lindeman, who in 1840 established on the neighbouring Paterson River the Cawarra vineyard that still gives its name to an Australian vintage. In 1847, however, twenty-three vignerons decided to introduce expert assistants from Europe. Of the seventy thus brought out King was responsible for three only; but from that time forth his product began to stand out. He was already president of the Hunter River Vineyard Association, and read papers before it year by year as well as letters received from notable growers in Europe. In 1850, and again in 1852, the Horticultural Society of Sydney awarded him gold medals for "light sparkling" and "white" wines, vintage of 1844; in 1854 he was requested to select for dispatch to the Paris Exhibition of 1855 a parcel of wines which achieved some renown—he gained a medal, his wines (along with those sent by William Macarthur) were chosen to appear on the table of the Emperor Napoleon III, and the Paris jury reported that his sparkling wines had "a bouquet, body and flavour equal to the finest champagnes." Even as a Parisian compliment that seems rather magnificent. Assuredly he deserved commendation, for he had spared no pains to attain high quality, had confined his annual production to about two thousand gallons, made from the grapes of four or five acres (larger crops, he said, resulted in inferior wine), and remained modest: "What I have there accomplished in the culture of the grape and making of wine can, under the same circumstances, be done by anybody."

He was still experimenting with sparkling wines when, in 1855, his health broke down and he was forced to make a round of the German spas. It became almost a triumphal tour. He was welcomed at Munich by Von Liebig, and by him passed on through Karlsbad and Wiesbaden to the Grand Duke of Nassau's Assmanshausen estates. There the Duke himself and his chief officials lavished praise on his work: "Your red wine is equal in all respects to that of Assmanshausen, which, as you know, holds the first rank among the Rhenish red wines. The white pattern, both for flavour and strength, rivals the best sorts of ours. It was only found to be 'firmer'—what we may render in English by the word 'riper'—than our wines usually are at such an early period." Nor was his fame confined to the Rhine valley; in 1856 *The Times* seems to have committed itself in a leading article to praise that promptly put up the price of Irrawang wines in the London market.

But it was too late for James King. He was a very sick man, and never saw Australia again. Instead, he made home to Edinburgh, and there in 1857 published a small pamphlet—*Australia may be an Extensive* WINE-GROWING *Country*—in which he related his experiences in order to encourage other growers. Why, said he, should the fast-increasing population (these were gold-rush days) poison itself with costly imported spirits when Australia could supply them with excellent light wines? The question has never been answered.

So James King passes out of history—but not his name, or his memory. Dead, he attained what one thinks must be an almost unique distinction. When he died we know not, but his widow married again; and her second husband, William Roberts of Penrith on the Nepean, left to the University of Sydney a sum of £4000 to found a scholarship in honour of the man he had succeeded. King's glass-sand and his potteries, his wines and his vineyards, sank into obscurity; their memory has been resuscitated only within the last few years. But the James King of Irrawang travelling scholarship, its origin forgotten even by the university that administers it, has provided for many brilliant Australian students of both sexes the chance of three years' study in Europe, and has thus trained—as it is still training—a remarkable succession of the native-born to fill professorial chairs in Australian universities.

INDEX

Aborigines, 17, 18
Age (newspaper), 101, 102, 106
Amboyna, 130, 136, 140
Amiens, Peace of, 168
Anna Josepha, brig, 168
Archer River, 133, 134
Arnhem, ship, 128, 130-3
Aru Islands, 130, 133, 137
Asschens, Lodewijk van, 140
Atlas (newspaper), 71
Australian (newspaper), 45, 185, 207
Australian Alps, 201

Baird, General David, 6
Ballarat, 112
Banda, 133
Banks, Sir Joseph, 143, 152, 154, 157, 170
Bannister, Saxe, 46
Bantam, 129
Barrallier, Francis, 156
Barrington, George, 37
Barton, Sir Edmund, 95, 98, 99, 110, 124
Bass, George, 156
Bass Strait, 197, 199, 200
Batavia, 128, 129, 135
Batavia River, 135
Batavia, ship, 128
Bath (Eng.), 179
Bathurst (N.S.W.), 10, 12, 14, 15, 84, 161, 163, 164, 200
Bathurst, Earl, 10, 13, 19, 20, 21, 23, 24, 25, 26, 28, 31, 32, 34, 163, 184
Bay of Islands (N.Z.), 170, 171, 172
Bayly, Nicholas, 22
Bent, Ellis, 21

Bent, Jeffery, 21, 24, 34
Berry, Alexander, 198, 199
Berry, Sir Graham, 102, 103, 104
Bigge, John Thomas, 13, 14, 22 n., 25, 27-8, 29, 30, 34, 44, 46, 168, 174, 176, 177, 183, 184, 185, 195, 199
Birmingham (Eng.), 67, 72
Blacktown (N.S.W.), 17
Blake, William 24-5
Bland, William, 48, 52, 55, 58, 72, 206
Blaxcell, Garnham, 12
Blaxland, Gregory, 10, 40, 42, 143-5, 147, 148, 151, 152, 154-65, 210
Blaxland, John, viii, 21, 22, 141-53, 154, 162, 165, 169, 178
Bligh, Governor, 4, 7, 8, 9, 18, 145, 146, 147, 148, 152, 153, 168, 169, 170, 171, 190, 192, 193
Blue Mountains, 10, 12, 40, 150, 155-64, 166, 198
Boswell, James, 5
Botany Bay, vi, viii, 154, 175, 209
Bourke, Governor, 50, 51, 205, 210
Boyd, ship, 170-2
Bright, John, 76
Brisbane, Governor, 22, 23, 30, 31, 45, 47, 151, 152, 193, 194, 198, 199, 204, 206, 207
Brisbane (Q.), 55, 141
Bristol (Eng.), 179
Broke (N.S.W.), 151
Broken Hill (N.S.W.), 93
Brothers, ship, 145, 197
Bruce, George, 171, 172

Index

Brush Farm (N.S.W.), 164
Buller, Charles, 49
Bulletin (newspaper), 98
Bulwer, Henry Lytton, 48
Bunyan, John, 100
Burragorang (N.S.W.), 198
Busby, James, 210

Caledon, Lord, 147
Caley, George, 157
Camden (N.S.W.), 15, 150
Campbell-Bannerman, Sir Henry, 119, 120
Carlyle, Thomas, 66, 76, 77
Carpentaria, Gulf of, 128, 129, 139
Carstenszoon, Jans, viii, 127-40, 203
Cartwright, Robert, 18
Castlereagh, Viscount, 4, 19
Casuarina tree, 173
Catastrophe, Cape, 137
Cawarra (N.S.W.), 211
Chaffey Brothers, 104
Chamberlain, Joseph, 110, 111
Chinese immigrants, 81, 86-7, 89
Churchill, Winston, 119
Cobden, Richard, 76
Cook, Captain James, v, viii, 128, 136, 138, 154
Cook, Sir Joseph, 121, 122
Cowper, Charles, 63, 76, 77, 80
Cox, William, 10, 163, 164

Dalley, William Bede, 76, 83, 84, 89
Dampier, William, 137-8
Darling, Governor, 30, 45, 46, 47, 48, 50, 57, 152, 204, 205
Davey, Lieutenant-Governor,167
Deakin, Alfred, vii, 96, 98-124
Dibbs, Sir George, 84, 88
Dickson, Sir James Robert, 110, 111
Diemen, Anthony van, 138, 139
Dilke, Sir Charles, 88-9
Drooge Bocht, 131, 132, 138, 139, 140
Duncan, Jonathan, 6

Duperrey, Commodore, 175, 207
Duyfken, yacht, 128-30, 135, 139

East India Company, the, v
Edwards, Major-General Bevan, 91
Elgin, Lord, 119
Empire (newspaper), 73, 74
Encounter Bay, 14, 197
Endeavour Strait, 136, 203
Evans, George William, 10, 14, 161-4
Experiment, brig, 172

False Cape, 130
Federation, Australian, 64, 80, 82, 90-6, 98, 107-11
Field, Barron, 44, 46, 177
Fisher, Andrew, 118, 121
FitzRoy, Governor, 54, 55
Fitzwilliam, Lord, 36, 39
Flinders, Matthew, 129
Forbes, Sir Francis, 45, 47
Forrest, Lord, 118
Forster, William, 71, 77
Foveaux, Colonel, 28, 176, 190
Fulton, Henry, 167
"Fusion," the, 118, 121
Fysh, Sir Philip, 110

Geelong (Vic.), 207
Gentleman's Magazine, 165-6
George's River, 154, 155
Gibbes, James, 71
Gilbert River, 132 n.
Gillies, Duncan, 91, 92, 107
Gipps, Governor, 50, 51, 53, 54, 55
Gladstone, William Ewart, 53, 67, 68, 80, 82, 83, 120
Goderich, Viscount, 209
Gonzal, Jean Etienne, 140
Goulburn, Henry, 23, 24, 27
Goulburn (N.S.W.), 15, 156
Goulburn River (N.S.W.), 155
Goulburn River (Vic.), 202
Grafton (N.S.W.), 186
Greenway, Francis Howard, 167, 179-86

Index

Gregory, Sir Augustus, 165
Grey, Earl, vi, 53, 54, 55, 59
Grose River, 156

Harpur, Charles, 71
Hashemy, ship, 55, 72
Hawkesbury River, 32, 155, 190, 202 n.
Hayes, Sir Henry Brown, 49–50
Heywood, John Pemberton, 36–7
Hobart (Tas.), 7, 9, 55
Hobson's Bay, 55
Hovell, William Henry, 172, 196–208
Howe, George, 187–95
Howe, Richard, 187
Howe, Robert, 195
Hullett brothers, 145
Hume, Hamilton, 15, 199–208
Hume, Joseph, 48
Hume River, 202, 206
Hunter, Governor, 16, 168, 187, 193
Hunter River, 54, 150, 151, 155, 164, 165, 186, 211
Hutchison, John, 173–4, 175, 178

Illawarra (N.S.W.), 15, 164
Irrawang (N.S.W.), 210
Irvine, Sir William, 118

Jamieson, Dr., 119
Jamison, Sir John, 49, 50, 52, 56, 57
Jansz, Willem, 129, 130, 131
Jaques, John, 189
Jardine River, 135, 136, 138
Jennings, Sir Patrick, 84
Johnson, Richard, 38, 39
Johnson, Dr. Samuel, 5
Johnston, Colonel, 147, 169, 171, 192

Kangaroo Island, 197, 198
Kanimbla Valley, 160
Kent, Thomas, 171, 172, 175–6, 178
Kiama, 77, 78, 79

King, Governor, 37, 144, 145, 171, 188, 189, 193
King, James, 209–13
King, Philip, 15 n.
Kingsley, Henry, 141
Kingston, Charles Cameron, 110, 111, 114, 124

"Labour," 95, 107, 113, 116, 117, 118, 121
Lachlan River, 14
Lake George, 15, 199, 200, 204
Lang, Dr., 62, 64
Laurier, Sir Wilfrid, 119
Lawson, Captain William, 40, 42, 157, 158, 161, 162, 164
Laycock, Lieutenant, 192
Leader (newspaper), 101
Leeuw, Arend Martensz de, 138
Leigh, Lord, 66
Lemmen, yacht, 139
Lennox, David, viii
Lesson, R. P., 35
Liebig, Baron von, 210, 212
Lindeman, Henry J., 211
Liverpool (N.S.W.), 13, 54
Liverpool (Eng.), 63, 76
Lord, Simeon, viii, 12, 18, 148, 167–78, 196, 197
Lowe, Robert, 54, 55, 57, 58, 62, 66, 71, 72, 73
Luddenham (Eng.), 142
Luddenham (N.S.W.), 150, 151

Macarthur, John, viii, 5, 21, 22, 23, 24, 27, 30, 34, 127, 141, 146, 147, 148, 149, 150, 152, 153, 156, 169, 190
Macarthur, Sir William, 211
Macleay, William Sharpe, 71
McMillan, Sir William, 113
Macquarie, Governor, vi, vii, 5–35, 37, 38, 39, 41, 44, 66, 96, 148, 149, 150, 152, 153, 157, 158, 161, 162, 163, 164, 166, 167, 169, 171–2, 173, 175, 176, 177, 179, 180, 181, 183, 184, 185, 186, 191, 193, 194
Macquarie, Mrs., 8, 33

Index

Macquarie River, 10, 14
MacQueen, Thomas, 192
Maitland (N.S.W.), 186
Maoris, the, 51, 169-71
Maribyrnong River, 202 n.
Marsden, Samuel, 14, 16, 20, 22, 24, 26, 34, 44, 141, 148, 171 n., 176, 184
Martin, Sir James, 39, 71, 77, 78, 79, 80
Matra, James Mario, v, vi
Mattarra. See Tarra
Mauritius, The, 168, 169
Meehan, Hugh, 168
Meehan, James, 15, 167
Michie, Sir Archibald, 71
Mildura (Vic.), 104
Mitchell, Sir Thomas, viii, 71
Mitchell Library, viii, 13, 33, 205
Mitchell River, 131
Molle, Colonel, 40, 176
Moor, James, 119
Moreton Bay, 28, 55
Mornington, Lord. See Wellesley-Pole
Morpeth (N.S.W.), 186
Mudgee (N.S.W.), 79
Murdoch, Walter, viii, 122, 123
Murray, David Christie, 92
Murray River, 15, 104, 151, 202
Murrumbidgee River, 14, 200, 201

Napoleon III, 211
Narellan (N.S.W.), 208
Nassau, Grand Duke of, 212
Nepean River, 18, 43, 148, 150, 158, 161, 202, 213
Newcastle, Duke of, 61
Newcastle (N.S.W.), 13, 28, 150, 151, 155, 209
New Guinea (see also Papua), 90, 104, 129, 130, 131, 137, 138, 139, 140
New Hebrides, 105
Newington (Eng.), 142, 143, 151
Newington (N.S.W.), 151, 165

New South Wales, vi, viii, 4, 7, 11, 15, 19, 20, 22 n., 23, 26, 27, 29, 31, 37, 38, 44, 47, 55, 60, 62, 72, 76, 79, 81, 83, 87, 90, 91, 93, 94, 95, 97, 108, 109, 110, 141, 142, 145, 150, 152, 153, 154, 167, 171, 179, 193, 194, 207, 211
New South Wales Corps, 3, 8, 146, 147, 157, 168
New Zealand, 22, 51, 91, 110, 119, 152, 169-70, 171, 172, 175, 197, 210
Nightingall, Major-General, 4-5
Norfolk Island, vi, 37, 38, 170
Northern Territory, 87, 116, 133 n.

O'Farrell, H. J., 78
Oxley, John, 14, 199

Pakington, Sir John, 56, 61, 76
Papua, 114, 128, 130, 137
Parkes, Sir Henry, vii, 55, 56, 57, 60, 62, 63, 64, 66-97, 99, 108
Parramatta (N.S.W.), 13, 16, 43, 54, 146, 181, 182, 189
Parry, Catherine, 38
Paterson River, 211
Pelsart, François, 128
Penrith (N.S.W.), 154, 158, 160, 161, 213
Pera, ship, 128, 130-6, 139
Phillip, Governor, viii, 20, 37, 154, 179, 183, 196
Phormium plant, 170-1
Pieterszoon, Pieter, 137
Piper, Captain John, 50
Polack, Andrew, 71
Pool, Gerrit Thomasz, 137
Porpoise, H.M.S., 7
Port Arthur, vi
Port Jackson, 3, 7, 12, 13, 15, 31, 33, 49, 69, 72, 87, 145, 155, 168, 179, 180, 184, 187, 196, 207
Port Macquarie, 15, 28
Port Musgrave, 131

Index

Port Phillip, 15, 59, 200, 203, 205, 207
Portadown (Ireland), 36
Praed, Winthrop Mackworth, 42, 43
Prince of Wales Island, 136, 138
Prospect (N.S.W.), 157, 161

Queensland, 75, 83, 90, 93, 110, 113 n., 141

Randolph, ship, 55
Rarotonga, 40
Read, Robert, 33
Redfern, William, 18, 27, 167
Reid, Sir George, 95, 96, 98, 99, 109, 113, 117, 118, 121
Riley, Alexander, 171, 172
Roberts, William, 213
Robertson, Sir John, 75, 76, 77, 79, 80, 82, 84, 89
Robinson, Michael, 167
Rumpf, Georg, 140

St. Kitts (W.I.), 187, 195
Salisbury, Lord, 105
Service, James, 92, 104
Sidmouth, Lord, 26
South Australia, 18, 83, 90, 93, 110, 116, 137, 141
Spencer Gulf, 198, 199, 204
Speult, Governor van, 130
Speult River, 135, 140
Stanley, Lord, 53
Statesman (newspaper), 44
Stephen, James, 192, 194
Strathfieldsaye, ship, 68, 69
Stuart, Sir Alexander, 82
Sturt, Captain Charles, 165, 197, 203, 206, 207
Sudan Expedition, 83, 89
Sydney (N.S.W.), 7, 8, 10, 11, 12, 13, 14, 16, 17, 23, 27, 37, 39, 40, 41, 44, 51, 52, 53 n., 54, 55, 61, 63, 69, 70, 72, 74, 77, 78, 79, 83, 87, 92, 93, 109, 144, 146, 148, 153, 155, 160, 165, 168, 170, 171, 175, 176, 179–85, 189, 191, 209, 210

Sydney Gazette (newspaper), 47, 185, 188–95
Sydney Morning Herald (newspaper), 69
Syme, David, 101, 102, 109
Syme, George, 101

Tarra, 170
Tasman, viii, 128, 133 n., 135, 138, 139, 140
Tasmania, v, 7, 9, 28, 39, 90, 110, 161, 164, 167, 175, 195, 197
Tennyson, Alfred Lord, 66, 82, 83 n.
Tenterfield (N.S.W.), 91
Te Pehi, 171, 172
Thompson, Andrew, 18, 172, 176
Thomson, Edward Deas, 54
Thornbury Castle (Eng.), 182, 184
Throsby, Charles, 15
Times, The (newspaper), 187, 191, 212
Trial, brig, 197
Torres, Luis Vaez de, 128, 137, 203
Trinidad (W.I.), 26, 27

University of Sydney, 58–9, 213

Vale, Benjamin, 23, 24, 25
Vaucluse (N.S.W.), 49, 50
Victoria (*see also* Port Phillip), v, 59, 83, 89, 90, 91, 93, 99, 101, 102, 103, 104, 105, 106, 108, 109, 110

Wakefield, Edward Gibbon, vi, 30, 42, 48–9, 51, 54, 60
Ward, Sir Joseph, 119
Wardell, Robert, 44–6, 48
Warragamba River, 18, 202 n.
Waterloo (N.S.W.), 209
Watson, John Christian, 117
Wellesley-Pole, William, 4
Wentworth, D'Arcy, 12, 18, 36–41

Index

Wentworth, William Charles, vi, vii, 34, 38–65, 66, 72, 73, 74, 75, 90, 95, 96, 158, 161, 162, 164, 185
Western Australia, 18, 111, 115, 141
Western Port (Vic.), 199, 200, 203, 204, 205, 206
Whangaroa (N.Z.), 170, 171
"White Australia" (*see also* Chinese), 85, 112, 113
Williams River, 209, 210
Wilson, John, 156
Wimborne (Eng.), 63

Windsor (N.S.W.), 13, 181
Wollombi (N.S.W.), 151
Wollondilly River, 155, 202
Wood, George Arnold, 127
Woolloomooloo (N.S.W.), 180
Wright, Captain, 204

Yarmouth (Eng.), 196
Yarra River, 200
Yass (N.S.W.), 200, 207
York, Cape, 136, 137
York, Mount, 160–1, 162, 163
Young, Sir George, v, vi